Mantra

Personal Guidance through the Power of the Word

By Bibiji Inderjit Kaur Khalsa, PhD

Kundalini Yoga as taught by Yogi Bhajan ®

Kundalini Research Institute

Training ❧ Publishing ❧ Research ❧ Resources

Mantra

Personal Guidance through the Power of the Word

© 2016 Bibiji Inderjit Kaur Khalsa

Published by the Kundalini Research Institute

Training ❀ Publishing ❀ Research ❀ Resources

PO Box 1819

Santa Cruz, NM 87567

www.kundaliniresearchinstitute.org

ISBN 978-1-934532-08-9

Creative Director: Rampreet Kaur

Project Editor: Rampreet Kaur

Copyeditor: Hargobind Hari Singh Khalsa, Shanti Kaur Khalsa, Sangeet Kaur Khalsa and Dr. Onkar Singh

Consulting Editors: Gurumeet Kaur Khalsa, Hargobind Hari Singh Khalsa

Author Photo: Lisa Law

Design and Layout: Prana Projects; Ditta Khalsa and Biljana Nedelkovska

The diet, exercise and lifestyle suggestions in this book come from ancient yogic traditions. Nothing in this book should be construed as medical advice. Any recipes mentioned herein may contain potent herbs, botanicals and naturally occurring ingredients which have traditionally been used to support the structure and function of the human body. Always check with your personal physician or licensed health care practitioner before making any significant modification in your diet or lifestyle, to insure that the ingredients or lifestyle changes are appropriate for your personal health condition and consistent with any medication you may be taking. For more information about Kundalini Yoga as taught by Yogi Bhajan® please see www.yogibhajan.org and www.kundaliniresearchinstitute.org.

Guru Ram Das
4th Sikh Guru
1534–1581

Dedication

This work is dedicated to spreading the healing light of Guru Ram Das, and to my beloved husband, Siri Singh Sahib Bhai Sahib Harbhajan Singh Khalsa Yogiji, who dedicated his life to serving the children of the Age of Aquarius as a humble disciple of his constant guide and Guru, Guru Ram Das. To all of the siblings of destiny who have committed themselves to the inner spiritual work of meditation on the Shabad Guru, that they shall serve and uplift humanity and all life upon our beautiful mother earth. Love and gratitude shall root out deception and greed and through the power of the Word we shall be ever protected by the living reality of the True Guru.

Contents

Table of Contents

Foreword

and Blessing from Yogi Bhajan for this Book

When I discussed this project with the
Siri Singh Sahib [Yogi Bhajan],
he said many important things about mantra,
which I am sharing with you in this foreword.

— Bibiji

Mantra is a code. It is a code to merge your mind with the infinite creative fire of life. *Man* means mind. *Tra* means life or creativity from Infinity. *Ra* means sun. When you recite mantra, you project the vibratory frequency of your own molecules into the Infinity of the Cosmos. That is mantra.

The power of mantra can tune your own consciousness into the awareness of the totality. By vibrating a mantra in rhythm with the breath, you can expand your sensitivity to the entire spectrum of vibration. Every element of the universe is in a constant state of vibration, manifesting to us as light, sound, and energy, which are the underlying frequencies that sustain all creation. Mantra teaches you to control the breath so that you can control your mind. Guru Nanak said, *Man Jeetai Jagjeet*. When you control your mind, you control the universe.

There are very clear scientific principles you must understand. Normally, a human perceives only a fraction of the infinite range of vibration. When you chant mantra, you expand and alter your conscious perception by changing the chemical composition of the fluids in the brain. There are eighty-four meridian points in the upper palate of the human mouth. You can feel the upper palate with the tongue, and while chanting, the tongue strokes and stimulates those meridian points. They in turn stimulate the hypothalamus, which makes the pineal gland radiate. When the pineal radiates, it creates a pulse in the pituitary gland and causes it to secrete, which activates the entire glandular system. Then the chemical composition of the brain becomes balanced and automatically changes your conscious perception and outlook on life. You may take every kind of drug imagined and unimagined, but nothing is equal to what your own system can produce.

As our planet completes its transition into the Age of Aquarius, every human being on this earth is impacted and must match up to a higher frequency. With many channels of realities in mega multiple manifestation, which every human being will have to face, the capacity of the mind will reach its optimum just dealing with everyday life. As the earth becomes smaller, human vitality must expand. Tides are turning and the world is calling for a greater capacity and caliber in a human. That time has come when our steel will be tested, so let us be ready to temper our steel. Mantra is the key.

Many will freak out, but those who discipline themselves to meditate each day will provide the life jacket to keep others afloat. The mind has to be sharp and clear, so just as we clean our bodies, we have to clean our mind each morning. Daily *japa,* or repetition of a mantra or sound current meditation, clears out the subconscious mind and balances the hemispheres of the brain, bringing compassion and patience.

When you sit to meditate, the subconscious mind *automatically* starts cleaning itself out. Thoughts which you have not been consciously aware of start appearing. Meditation and daydreaming are not two different things. Let the thoughts come, but see that the rhythm of the mantra is continuously there. Even fantasizing in meditation can be creatively positive if you do *japa* with it. Keep on cutting the fantasies with a mantra and your mind will be clean. Meditation with a mantra is nothing but *creatively conscious* daydreaming. Any thought which you can pass through that meditation and cut with a mantra will never occur in your life with any negative effect.

God has given us the *Word* so we can know how to balance the energy of our subtle bodies and overcome hazard and misfortune, which are only a result of dips or depression in the flow of life. Reciting mantra brings clarity, inner strength, balance, and vitality in life to honor our own word. If your words have the strength of the Infinite in them and are virtuous, and you value them, you are the greatest of the great. If you do not value your words, you have no value. Your own word is your value as a human being.

We are living in the *Kali Yug*, known as the Age of Darkness or the machine age, which means truth is only one quarter revealed in a sea of deceit and many lies. By reciting mantra, we can cut through falsehood and shield our being to be victorious. To recognize what is true, chant these mantras to align yourself with your own infinity and remain true to the purity of your own soul. Nothing and no one can deceive you, and you will shine as bright as a lighthouse in the night to guide the way.

The hand of Guru shall work in the lives of all those who serve and uplift others and Guru shall give the grace to know the way, even at hard times in life. By reciting mantra, we are uplifted from all human suffering and are able to intuitively prepare for or avoid encountering unfavorable circumstances, times, or psyches that may otherwise be experienced as conflict in our lives. We can then face events in such a way that we shall excel, succeed, and become victorious. There is no substitute for victory, that is why we say, *Wahe Guru Ji Ka Khalsa, Wahe Guru Ji Ki Fateh.*

Blessing

We have had the privilege and blessing to compile these mantras. When used correctly, mantra brings liberation and unites the being with the Divine. I am grateful to God and Guru that all of her life, Bibiji has chanted God's Name. She relies only upon the Siri Guru Granth Sahib as her sole source of solace, strength, and support and looks to no other. We, as spiritual beings in this earthly realm, believe in the unity of all humankind as the highest order of existence and that a person of any religious doctrine, whether it be Jewish, Muslim, Christian, Buddhist, Hindu, etc., can always use this knowledge. The sound current is a universal tool for all people to be protected and promoted to victory.

Siri Singh Sahib Bhai Sahib Harbhajan Singh Khalsa Yogiji

Introduction to Mantra

The Nature of Sound

"Every element of the universe is in a constant state of vibration manifested to us as light, sound, and energy. The human senses perceive only a fraction of the infinite range of vibration, so it is difficult to comprehend that the Word mentioned in the Bible is actually the totality of vibration which underlies and sustains all creation. A person can tune his or her own consciousness into the awareness of that totality with the use of a mantra. By vibrating in rhythm with the breath to a particular sound that is proportional to the creative sound, or sound current, one can expand one's sensitivity to the entire spectrum of vibration. It is similar to striking a note on a stringed instrument. In other words, as you vibrate, the universe vibrates with you."

– Yogi Bhajan

We live in a sea of energy. Energy vibrates. Everything in the manifest creation is vibrating. Even seemingly solid, inanimate objects are constantly vibrating, simply vibrating at a slower or lower frequency than animate objects. Some vibrations are audible — sounds we can hear with our ears. Thoughts are silent sounds, electromagnetic vibrations. The higher the frequency, the less dense and more etheric the quality of the vibration we hear and speak, the more our own vibrational frequency is raised. Raising our own vibration brings us closer to experiencing and merging with the highest vibration of all — God — the original creativity of the universe.

The entire universe was built on sound, on vibration. Putting it poetically: God spoke, and the world came into being. More precisely, God vibrated, and all the universes and worlds, solar systems, oceans, land, and sky, and the myriad of beings that inhabit them appeared. There is a vibratory frequency that corresponds to everything in the universe. By vibrating a particular combination of sounds, you tune into various levels of intelligence, or consciousness. Situations, people, and events respond to the signals you send out. The vibratory frequency of a mantra draws to you whatever you are vibrating.

Chanting Mantras

Chanting mantras, either silently or out loud, is a conscious method of controlling and directing the mind. Happiness, sorrow, joy, and regret are vibratory frequencies in the mind. Call them attitudes or beliefs, but fundamentally, they are vibratory frequencies or thought waves. They determine the kind of program our mind plays. The scenario we choose becomes our vibration, defines how we feel and what we project to others. We can exercise our right to choose at any time.

We are creating with every word we speak, and even with every word we think. When we chant a mantra we are choosing to invoke the positive power contained in those particular syllables. Whether it's for prosperity, peace of mind, increasing intuition, or any of the other multitude of possible benefits inherent in mantras, simply by chanting them we are setting vibrations into motion that shall have an effect. It doesn't actually matter if we understand the meaning of the sounds or not.

(From Kundalini Yoga: The Flow of Eternal Power by ShaktiParwha Kaur Khalsa)

The Science of Naad Yoga

Why Chanting Works

Naad is a process of harmony through which the *aad*, the Infinite, can be experienced. *Naad* is the basic sound for all languages through all times. This sound comes from one common source or sound current. It is the universal code behind language and therefore behind human communication.

The science of Naad Yoga is thousands of years old. It works with the movement of the tongue in the mouth, language, and chemical changes in the brain. There is no system of nerve connections between the sections of the brain—no wiring. Rather, there is a neurotransmission fluid. Different chemical liquids are secreted from different parts of the brain. Messages are transmitted from each part of the brain through the fluids, which are called *naad namodam rasaa*. *Naad* refers to communicating harmony; *namodam* means addressing; and *rasaa* means juice.

We can alter consciousness by changing the chemical composition of the brain fluids. The state of mind, personality, and power to project from our authentic self is impacted by the use of our word.

> "If your words have the strength of the Infinite in them and are virtuous, and you value them, you are the greatest of the great. If you do not value your words, you have no value. Your own word is your value as a human being. Your word is your value."
>
> – *Yogi Bhajan, The Teachings of Yogi Bhajan*

Merger through the Word

There are two caves *(gupha)* in the body which generate through the creative process. One is the *bij gupha* or seed cave, which relates to the male and female sexual organs. The other is the *gian gupha* or cave of knowledge, which relates to the tongue and mouth. The science of Naad Yoga is concerned with the *gian gupha*, in which the movement of the tongue in the mouth while chanting is likened to the male and female sexual organs in the *bij gupha*. It creates the experience of merger with the Divine.

Three Voices of Mantra

Mantras are chanted in three different voices, each with a specific purpose. Chanting aloud trains the mind and nervous system to experience the physiological changes imparted by rhythm and breath during recitation. The second voice, a whisper, invokes a direct connection to your soul. The third voice is ultimately the most powerful vibration, a focused thought projection ("mentally vibrating" a sound). It is good to practice chanting aloud in order to control the mind and thoughts and learn to remain focused on the mantra before chanting with the voice of mental vibration, the *Voice of the Divine*.

The Three Voices of Mantra:

Voice of the Human

Chanting in a normal voice

Voice of the Beloved

Chanting in a whisper

Voice of the Divine

Chanting silently

Meditation effects for the amount of time you meditate:

Meditating for 3 minutes alters the electromagnetic field, the circulation, and stability of the blood.

Meditating for 7 minutes begins to shift brain patterns and the magnetic field surrounding the body increases in strength.

Meditating for 11 minutes begins to change the nervous and glandular systems.

Meditating for 22 minutes allows the three minds, i.e., the negative, positive, and neutral minds, to come into balance and begin to work together. The subconscious mind begins to clear.

Meditating for 31 minutes allows the glands, breath, and concentration to affect all the cells and rhythms of the body. Endocrine secretions are completely balanced as is the ethereal energy of *the chakras* (junction points of physical and spiritual centers).

Meditating for 62 minutes changes the gray matter in the brain. It stimulates the frontal lobe of the brain as well as the pituitary and pineal glands. You work through the physical body, emotions and mental states and communicate with aspects of the Divine within yourself. The subconscious "shadow mind" and the outer projections become integrated.

Meditating for 2 ½ hours changes the psyche in its correlation with the surrounding magnetic field so that the subconscious mind is held firmly in the new pattern by the surrounding Universal Mind. You totally remake your psyche. These changes persist throughout the day and are reflected by positive changes in mood and behavior.

In the Piscean Age that we have now left behind, it was a central and even sacred task to find and gain access to information. The motto of the age was, "to be or not to be." Learn, grow, and become something. Great knowledge about human potential was guarded by secrecy and layers of initiations. The Piscean Age was dominated by machines and hierarchies. As the new Aquarian Age dawns, the old defenses and manipulations based on hiding and controlling access to information will no longer work.

Meditation effects for the number of days that you meditate:

40 days to break a habit.

90 days to gain the new habit.

120 days and you are the new habit.

1,000 days and you are the Master of it.

Gurmukhi Script – The Language of Mantra

Mantras come in every language and all mantras serve to awaken our divine consciousness. Many of the mantras in this compilation come from the sacred language of the Sikhs known as Gurmukhi, or from the mouth of the Guru. Gurmukhi is considered a sacred text because it is not used for any other purpose than to exalt the Infinite and awaken our divine nature. The Gurmukhi sound current transcends religious beliefs and embodies universal truths.

The hymns and verses written in Gurmukhi are called Gurbani, or the words of the Guru.

Pronunciation Guide

Gurbani is a sophisticated sound system with guidelines for pronunciation and other rules of the language that are best conveyed through a direct student-teacher relationship. The Gurmukhi alphabet and vowels are shown below. Further guidelines regarding pronunciation are available at *www.kundaliniresearchinstitute.org*.

> Audio to assist with pronunciation of all mantras in this book is available at the Kundalini Research Institute's online store. Please visit KRI's store via the homepage: www.kundaliniresearchinstitute.org

ੳ	ਅ	ੲ	ਸ	ਹ	ਕ	ਖ	ਗ
ooraa	airaa	eeree	sasa	haha	kaka	khakha	gaga
ਘ	ਙ	ਚ	ਛ	ਜ	ਝ	ਞ	ਟ
ghagha	nanga	chacha	chhachha	jaja	jhajha	nyanya	tainka
ਠ	ਡ	ਢ	ਣ	ਤ	ਥ	ਦ	ਧ
thatha	dada	dhadha	nana	tata	thatha	dada	dhadha
ਨ	ਪ	ਫ	ਬ	ਭ	ਮ	ਯ	ਰ
nana	papa	phapha	baba	bhabha	mama	yeye	rara
ਲ	ਵ	ੜ	ਸ਼	ਖ਼	ਗ਼	ਜ਼	ਫ਼
lala	vawa	rara	shasha	khakha	ghagha	zaza	fafa

Gurmukhi Vowels

ੀ	'ee' as in seen
ੂ	'oo' as in soon
ੇ	'ay' as in say
ਾ	'aa' as in calm
ੈ	'ai' as in happy
ੋ	'o' as in so
ੌ	'ou' as in bought
	'a' as in about *
ਿ	'i' as in win (pronounced sometimes)
ਿ	'e' as in ache (silent sometimes)
ੁ	'u' as in put

*The 'a' vowel sound (mukta) is assumed and not denoted in Gurmukhi.

A Brief History of Gurmukhi

Gurmukhi means *"from the mouth of the Guru."* Guru Angad, the second Sikh Guru, organized the Gurmukhi alphabet. The availability of this simple script accomplished something very special by allowing all people to learn to read and pronounce the songs written by Guru Nanak. Up until that point in the history of the region, written language was reserved only for the powerful and the wealthy of high castes. Written language simply was not available to common people.

Gurmukhi was developed to be a simple, clear, and very precise phonetic language. By learning to pronounce Gurmukhi script, people were able to learn to read and correctly pronounce the songs, as they were spoken by Guru Nanak. Guru Nanak, and the Sikh Gurus who followed him, also preserved songs of other masters and sages from different religions. The development of Gurmukhi was key to opening the doors of the Shabad Guru to all people. Gurmukhi is a great blessing and divine gift to all humanity, so everyone is able to experience reciting and singing sacred songs and verses that were previously kept secret from them. By learning this very simple method of pronunciation and repeating the words of the sages, you begin to induce in yourself the same state of consciousness that they were in when they sang the songs. It begins to create the same changes in the physiology. It opens doors to higher awareness and all that is required is that your breath and voice imitate and repeat those sounds.

Kundalini Yoga

As Taught By Yogi Bhajan®

Kundalini Yoga

From *Lectures and Conversations with Yogi Bhajan, 1969*

I have recognized, with the blessing of my Master, that it is possible to be healthy, to be happy, and to be holy while living in this society; but you must have energy so that your dead computer may live and pass on the signal to you and compute all that you want to do. We call this energy, in the old science, the Kundalini, which has been blocked in the *Mooladhara*, the lowest of all chakras or lotuses.

These are all imaginary things. Great big books have been written on them and these books also misled me for many years. Still I learned about it, and all these chakras (or circles as we call them in English), have put us in so many circles that we do not come out of it and we reach nowhere. There is a way we should set our computer to be in direct contact with Him, the Biggest Computer, and all things must then work automatically. That cannot work until the Kundalini, the spiritual nerve, breaks through the blockage at the Mooladhara and travels up, reaching the stage where you may have superconsciousness in consciousness.

You must generate the pressure of the praana and mix it with the apaana, and thus, when the two join together, you generate heat in the praanic center. With this heat of the praana, you put a pressure or charge on the Kundalini, the soul nerve, which is coiled in three and a half circles on the Mooladhara. "Kundal" means "the curl of the hair of the beloved." It does not mean snake or serpent. This will awaken it so that it may pierce through the imaginary chakras and pass ultimately through *Jalandhara Bandha* (neck lock — the final blockage in the spine before the energy reaches the head).

Now, let me define a few terms. *Praana* is the life force of the atom. *Apaana* is elimination or the eliminating force. These are two forces, positive and negative, in us which are governed by *pingala* and *ida*; that is, right and left. When we join these two energies under the power and the science of Kundalini Yoga, we mix the praana with the apaana and, under that pressure, bring up the Kundalini. When it passes through the central nerve or shushmuna, it reaches the higher chakras or lotuses, and thus man can easily look into the future. His psychic power becomes activated. He can know his total surroundings and he is a blessed being.

After one inhales the praana deep (down to the Navel Point) and pulls the apaana with the root lock (up to the Navel Point), praana and apaana mix at the Navel Center. This is known as *Nabhi Chakra* at the fourth vertebra. Heat is felt during the Kundalini awakening and that heat is the filament of the shushmuna or central spinal channel being lit by the joining of praana and apaana. Below the Nabhi Chakra, the energy leaves the navel and goes to the rectum (or lower center) and then it rises. This is called reserve channels. It relates to your astral body.

Then there are six more chakras through which the Kundalini must rise — and it will happen all at once. Once you have raised it, that's it. The hardest job is to keep it up, to keep the channels clean and clear.

From the rectum to the vocal cord is known as the silver cord. From the neck to the top of the head is the passage. From the third eye to the pineal gland is the gold cord. To make the energy rise in these cords and passages, you must apply hydraulic locks. You must put a pressure. You live in California? You know how we take the oil out of the ground? Put a pressure and the oil will come out. Your spine is a staircase of energy. 1) Mool Bandh brings apaana, eliminating force, to the navel and fourth vertebra, the central seat of the Kundalini. 2) Diaphragm Lock takes it to the neck. 3) Neck Lock takes it up all the rest of the way.

The pineal gland, or seat of the soul, does not work when the tenth gate (top of the head) is sealed, but if the pineal will secrete (when the Kundalini heat comes), your pituitary will act as radar, keeping the mind from negativity.

Yes, Kundalini is known as the nerve of the soul. This is to be awakened. Your soul is to be awakened. When the soul gets awakened, there remains nothing. What else is there?

In the practical reality, these chakras are imaginary and nothing else. This Kundalini is just a Kundalini and nothing else. It is not very important. These praanas and apaanas are just there. Everything is set in us. We lack nothing. We use these terms simply to make the process clear so we can get on with it. It is very simple. After getting myself into the darkness for many years, I found that if I would have known on the first day that it was so easy, I could have saved myself a lot of hassle. When I found out that the Kundalini really can come up like this, I was astonished. It was a surprise to me. I said, "That's all there is to the Kundalini?" and my Master said, "Yes."

About Yogi Bhajan

Born Harbhajan Singh Puri, August 26, 1929, in the part of India that became Pakistan in 1948, he was the son of a medical doctor. He spent his youth in privileged environments in private schools and his summers in the exclusive Dalhousie mountain region of Himachal Pradesh. As a young boy he attended a Catholic convent school.

> **"If you can't see God in all,**
> **you can't see God at all."**

When he was just eight years old he began his yogic training with an enlightened teacher, Sant Hazara Singh. His teacher proclaimed Yogi Bhajan a Master of Kundalini Yoga when he was sixteen years old.
He married Inderjit Kaur in 1952. They had two sons, Ranbir Singh and Kulbir Singh, and a daughter, Kamaljit Kaur.

In September of 1968, he left India for Canada to teach yoga at the University of Toronto. After two months in Canada, he flew to Los Angeles for a weekend visit. Arriving in Los Angeles virtually unknown, Yogi Bhajan met a number of young hippies, the spiritual seekers of that era. He immediately recognized that the experience of higher consciousness they were attempting to find through drugs could be achieved by practicing the Science of Kundalini Yoga, while simultaneously rebuilding their nervous systems. Breaking the centuries-old tradition of secrecy surrounding the empowering science of Kundalini Yoga, he began teaching it publicly.

From humble beginnings, teaching first at the East West Cultural Center and then in a student's furniture store in West Hollywood, the "Yogi" was like a magnet. Students flocked to his classes. Soon he was teaching at colleges and universities, including Claremont and UCLA, and accepting invitations to teach in other cities.

**"It's not the life that matters,
it's the courage that you bring to it."**

Yogi Bhajan crusaded tirelessly to educate, uplift, and enlighten everyone he met. His basic message was "It is your birthright to be healthy, happy, and holy". Embodying a rare combination of spiritual and down-to-earth practical wisdom, Yogi Bhajan was equally at home at the pulpit or podium, in the board room or living room, or sitting on a grassy lawn teaching and educating people of all walks of life. His expertise and influence extended into the realms of communication, healing arts, business, religion, and government.

**"Don't love me, love my teachings.
Become ten times greater than me."**

Although Yogi Bhajan has left his physical form, he asked that his students and those who knew him celebrate his homecoming. The light of his spiritual essence continues to bless all those whom he loved, and that is the entire human race.

Keys to Successful Practice

from the Kundalini Research Institute

Beginning Your Practice — Tuning In

The practice of Kundalini Yoga as taught by Yogi Bhajan® always begins with "tuning in." This simple practice of chanting the Adi Mantra 3-5 times aligns your mind, your spirit, and your body to become alert and assert your will so that your practice will fulfill its intention. It's a simple bowing to your Higher Self and an alignment with the teacher within. The mantra may be simple but it links you to a Golden Chain of teachers, an entire body of consciousness that guides and protects your practice: *Ong Namo Guroo Dayv Namo,* which means, "I bow to the Infinite, I bow to the Teacher within."

ONG	NAMO	GURU	DEV	NAMO
(rhymes with cone)	(rhymes with cosmo)	(rhymes with boohoo)	(sounds like Dave)	(rhymes with cosmo)
Infinite Creator	I Bow	Wisdom	Subtle Energy	I Bow

Ong---   Na-mo---   Gu-ru Dev---   Namo---

How to End Your Practice

Another tradition within Kundalini Yoga as taught by Yogi Bhajan® is a simple blessing known as *The Long Time Sun Shine Song*. Sung or simply recited at the end of your practice, it allows you to dedicate your practice to all those who've preserved and delivered these teachings so that you might have the experience of your Self. It is a simple prayer to bless yourself and others. It completes the practice and allows your entire discipline to become a prayer, in service to the good of all.

May the long time sun shine upon you

All love surround you

And the pure light within you

Guide your way on.

Sat Naam.

Other Tips for a Successful Experience

Prepare for your practice by lining up all the elements that will elevate your experience: natural fiber clothing and head covering (cotton or linen), preferably white to increase your auric body; natural fiber mat of either cotton or wool. Traditionally a sheep skin or other animal skin is used. If you have to use a rubber or petroleum-based mat, cover the surface with a cotton or wool blanket to protect and support your electromagnetic field. Clean air and fresh water also helps support your practice.

Once you have selected a mantra for your meditation practice, keep up for 40 days to experience the results.

Practice in Community

Studying the science of Kundalini Yoga with a KRI certified teacher can enhance your experience and deepen your understanding of kriya, mantra, breath, and posture. Find a teacher in your area at the International Kundalini Yoga Teachers Association website *www.ikyta.org*. If you are interested in becoming a teacher of Kundalini Yoga as taught by Yogi Bhajan®, go to *www.kundaliniresearchinstitute.org* for more information. Aquarian Teacher Trainings take place year-round all over the world!

Clarity

Charan Sat Sat Parsanhaar

Guru Arjan Dev Ji
Raag Gauree
SGGS 285

ਚਰਨ ਸਤਿ ਸਤਿ ਪਰਸਨਹਾਰ ॥
Charan sat sat parsanhaar

ਪੂਜਾ ਸਤਿ ਸਤਿ ਸੇਵਦਾਰ ॥
Poojaa sat sat sevadaar

ਦਰਸਨੁ ਸਤਿ ਸਤਿ ਪੇਖਨਹਾਰ ॥
Darshan sat sat paykhanhaar

ਨਾਮੁ ਸਤਿ ਸਤਿ ਧਿਆਵਨਹਾਰ ॥
Naam sat sat dhiaavanhaar

ਆਪਿ ਸਤਿ ਸਤਿ ਸਭ ਧਾਰੀ ॥
Aap sat sat sabh dhaaree

ਆਪੇ ਗੁਣ ਆਪੇ ਗੁਣਕਾਰੀ ॥
Aapay gun aapay gunkaaree

ਸਬਦੁ ਸਤਿ ਸਤਿ ਪ੍ਰਭੁ ਬਕਤਾ ॥
Shabad sat sat prabh baktaa

ਸੁਰਤਿ ਸਤਿ ਸਤਿ ਜਸੁ ਸੁਨਤਾ ॥
Surat sat sat jas sunataa

ਬੁਝਨਹਾਰ ਕਉ ਸਤਿ ਸਭ ਹੋਇ ॥
Bujhanhaar kao sat sabh hoi

ਨਾਨਕ ਸਤਿ ਸਤਿ ਪ੍ਰਭੁ ਸੋਇ ॥
Naanak sat sat prabh soi

His lotus feet are true,
and true are those who touch them.

His devotional worship is true,
and true are those who worship Him.

The blessing of His vision is true,
and true are those who behold it.

His Name is true,
and true are those who meditate on it.

He Himself is true,
and true is all that He sustains.

He Himself is virtuous goodness,
and he Himself is the bestower of virtue.

The word of His Shabad is true,
and true are those who speak of God.

Those ears are true,
and true are those who listen to His praises.

All is true to one who understands.

O Nanak, true, true is He, the Lord God.

From the *Siri Guru Granth Sahib*, Sukhmani Sahib,
Guru Arjun Dev Ji.

Clarity: Gives you the consciousness to discern
truthfulness from deception and unites you with
the Infinite within you.

Jeean Kaa Daataa Ayk Hai

Guru Arjan Dev Ji
Raag Bilaaval
818

ਜੀਅਨ ਕਾ ਦਾਤਾ ਏਕੁ ਹੈ ਬੀਆ ਨਹੀ ਹੋਰੁ॥
Jeean kaa daataa ayk hai beeaa nahee hor

The One Lord is the Giver for all beings;
there is no other at all.

Neutrality: Takes away duality and negative ego.

Jo Too Kareh

Guru Arjan Dev Ji
Raag Dhanaasree
677

ਜੋ ਤੂ ਕਰਹਿ ਕਰਾਵਹਿ ਸੁਆਮੀ ਸਾ ਮਸਲਤਿ ਪਰਵਾਣੁ ॥
Jo too kareh karaaveh suaamee saa maslat parvaan

Whatever You do, or cause to be done,
O Lord and Master,
that outcome is acceptable to me.

Neutrality: Brings realization of infinity
and takes away duality.

Sarbang Hantaa

ਸਰਬੰ ਹੰਤਾ॥ ਸਰਬੰ ਗੰਤਾ॥
Sarbang hantaa, sarbang gantaa

ਸਰਬੰ ਖਿਆਤਾ॥ ਸਰਬੰ ਗਿਆਤਾ॥
Sarbang khiaataa, sarbang giaataa

ਸਰਬੰ ਹਰਤਾ॥ ਸਰਬੰ ਕਰਤਾ॥
Sarbang hartaa, sarbang kartaa

ਸਰਬੰ ਪ੍ਰਾਣੰ॥ ਸਰਬੰ ਤ੍ਰਾਣੰ॥
Sarbang praanang, sarbang traanang

ਸਰਬੰ ਕਰਮੰ॥ ਸਰਬੰ ਧਰਮੰ॥
Sarbang karmang, sarbang dharmang

ਸਰਬੰ ਜੁਗਤਾ॥ ਸਰਬੰ ਮੁਕਤਾ॥
Sarbang jugtaa, sarbang muktaa

O Lord, You are the Destroyer of all.
You can reach all creatures,
and are well known to them.
You know the inner feelings of everyone.

O Lord, it is You who takes the
life back from creatures and
it is You, who gives them life.
You are the very life of everyone,
and You are the power behind all.

O Lord, being present in all,
it is You alone who does all deeds,
and takes responsibility for righteousness (Dharma).
Although you are present in all creatures,
You are distinctly unique.

This mantra comes from Jaap Sahib, the
beginning prayer in the *Dasam Granth* of the
Tenth Sikh Master, Guru Gobind Singh.

Neutrality: Develops the neutral mind
and dispels false beliefs and illusion
emanating from irrational fears.

Contentment

Aoukhee Gharee Na Daykhan Dayee

Guru Arjan Dev Ji
Raag Dhanaasree
682

ਅਉਖੀ ਘੜੀ ਨ ਦੇਖਣ ਦੇਈ ਅਪਨਾ ਬਿਰਦੁ ਸਮਾਲੇ॥
Aoukhee gharee na daykhan dayee apanaa birad samaalay

ਹਾਥ ਦੇਇ ਰਾਖੈ ਅਪਨੇ ਕਉ ਸਾਸਿ ਸਾਸਿ ਪ੍ਰਤਿਪਾਲੇ॥
Haath dayai raakhai apunay kou saas saas pratipaalay

The Divine Master does not let
the devotee see difficult times.
This is innate and natural.

The hand of protection shields the devotee;
with each and every breath taken,
the devotee is cherished and protected.

Contentment: Brings contentment and graceful surroundings.

Baah Pakar Prabh Kaadhei-aa

Guru Arjan Dev Ji
Raag Bilaaval
817

ਬਾਹ ਪਕੜਿ ਪ੍ਰਭਿ ਕਾਢਿਆ ਕੀਨਾ ਅਪਨਇਆ ॥
Baah pakar prabh kaadhei-aa keenaa apanei-aa

ਸਿਮਰਿ ਸਿਮਰਿ ਮਨ ਤਨ ਸੁਖੀ ਨਾਨਕ ਨਿਰਭਇਆ ॥
Simar simar man tan sukhee Naanak nirbhei-aa

Grabbing hold of my arm,
God has pulled me up and out;
He has made me His own.

Meditating, meditating in remembrance,
my mind and body are at peace;
Nanak has become fearless.

Contentment: To overcome depression and
negative thinking.

Daas Tayray Kee Bayntee

Guru Arjan Dev Ji
Raag Bilaaval
SGGS page 818

ਦਾਸ ਤੇਰੇ ਕੀ ਬੇਨਤੀ ਰਿਦ ਕਰਿ ਪਰਗਾਸੁ ॥
Daas tayray kee bayntee rid kar pargaas

This is the prayer of Your slave.
Please enlighten my heart.

Contentment: Brings radiance through clarity of heart and mind.

Jis Hath Jor Kar Vaykhai So-ei

Guru Nanak Dev Ji
Japji Sahib
SGGS page 7

ਜਿਸੁ ਹਥਿ ਜੋਰੁ ਕਰਿ ਵੇਖੈ ਸੋਇ॥
Jis hath jor kar vaykhai so-ei

ਨਾਨਕ ਉਤਮੁ ਨੀਚੁ ਨ ਕੋਇ॥
Naanak uttam neech na ko-ei

The Lord, who is all powerful,
creates everything and takes care of the creation.

Nanak, there is none high and none low.

Contentment: Destroys negative thinking patterns
and destructive behavior.

Karo Baynantee Sunhu Mayray Meetaa

Guru Arjan Dev Ji
Sohila
13

ਕਰਉ ਬੇਨੰਤੀ ਸੁਣਹੁ ਮੇਰੇ ਮੀਤਾ ਸੰਤ ਟਹਲ ਕੀ ਬੇਲਾ॥
Karo baynantee sunhu mayray meetaa sant tahal kee baylaa

ਈਹਾ ਖਾਟਿ ਚਲਹੁ ਹਰਿ ਲਾਹਾ ਆਗੈ ਬਸਨੁ ਸੁਹੇਲਾ॥
Eehaa khaat chalhu har laahaa aagai basan suhaylaa

Friends, listen to what I say.
Now is the time, in this life, to serve the saints.

Recite the Name in this world,
so that you stay in peace in the next world, after death.

Contentment: Dispels the pain of separation and loneliness.

Mayray Man Mukh Har Har Har Bolee-ai

Guru Raam Daas Ji
Raag Dayv Gandhaaree
527

ਮੇਰੇ ਮਨ ਮੁਖਿ ਹਰਿ ਹਰਿ ਹਰਿ ਬੋਲੀਐ ॥

Mayray man mukh har har har bolee-ai

ਗੁਰਮੁਖਿ ਰੰਗਿ ਚਲੂਲੈ ਰਾਤੀ ਹਰਿ ਪ੍ਰੇਮ ਭੀਨੀ ਚੋਲੀਐ ॥ ਰਹਾਉ ॥

Gurmukh rang chaloolai raatee har
praym bheenee cholee-ai (Rahaao)

ਹਉ ਫਿਰਉ ਦਿਵਾਨੀ ਆਵਲ ਬਾਵਲ ਤਿਸੁ ਕਾਰਨਿ ਹਰਿ ਢੋਲੀਐ ॥

Hao firao divaanee aaval baaval tis kaaran har dholee-ai

ਕੋਈ ਮੇਲੈ ਮੇਰਾ ਪ੍ਰੀਤਮੁ ਪਿਆਰਾ ਹਮ ਤਿਸ ਕੀ ਗੁਲ ਗੋਲੀਐ ॥

Koee maylai mayraa preetam piaaraa ham tis kee gul golee-ai

ਸਤਿਗੁਰੁ ਪੁਰਖੁ ਮਨਾਵਹੁ ਅਪੁਨਾ ਹਰਿ ਅੰਮ੍ਰਿਤੁ ਪੀ ਝੋਲੀਐ ॥

Satgur purkh manaavho apunaa har amrit pee jholee-ai

ਗੁਰ ਪ੍ਰਸਾਦਿ ਜਨ ਨਾਨਕ ਪਾਇਆ ਹਰਿ ਲਾਧਾ ਦੇਹ ਟੋਲੀਐ ॥

Gur parsaad jan Naanak paaei-aa har laadhaa dayh tolee-ai

Mantra

O my mind, chant the Name of the Lord, Har, Har, Har.

The Gurmukh is imbued with the deep red color of the poppy.
His shawl is saturated with the Lord's Love. Pause

I wander around here and there, like a madman,
bewildered, seeking out my Darling Lord.

I shall be the slave of the slave of whoever
unites me with my Darling Beloved.

So align yourself with the Almighty True Guru;
drink in and savor the Ambrosial Nectar of the Lord.

By Guru's Grace, servant Nanak has obtained
the wealth of the Lord within.

Contentment: Develops strength and contentment
through surrendering our finite self to the Infinite
Divine will.

Naanak Naam Dhiaa-ei-aa

Guru Arjan Dev Ji
Raag Sorath
625

ਨਾਨਕ ਨਾਮੁ ਧਿਆਇਆ
Naanak naam dhiaa-ei-aa

ਆਦਿ ਪੁਰਖ ਪ੍ਰਭੁ ਪਾਇਆ ॥
Aad purkh prabh paaei-aa

Nanak meditates on the Name.

The Primal Being is found in the light within.

Contentment: To create a meditative mind.

Saas Saas Man Naam

Guru Arjan Dev Ji
Raag Dhanaasree
673

ਸਾਸਿ ਸਾਸਿ ਮਨੁ ਨਾਮੁ ਸਮ੍ਹਾਰੈ
Saas Saas man naam samaarai

ਇਹੁ ਬਿਸ੍ਰਾਮ ਨਿਧਿ ਪਾਈ ॥
Eiho bisraam nidh paa-ee

With each and every breath,
my mind remembers the Name of the Divine.

In this way it finds the treasure of Peace.

Contentment: To remember with each and every breath the Name of the Divine.

Chanting the Name without ceasing is the way to find the treasure of bliss. The eternal Divine presence is found within.

Divine Mother

Bhand Jammee-ai

Guru Nanak Dev Ji
Raag Aasaa
473

ਭੰਡਿ ਜੰਮੀਐ ਭੰਡਿ ਨਿੰਮੀਐ ਭੰਡਿ ਮੰਗਣੁ ਵੀਆਹੁ॥
Bhand jammee-ai bhand nimmee-ai bhand mangan veeaaho

ਭੰਡਹੁ ਹੋਵੈ ਦੋਸਤੀ ਭੰਡਹੁ ਚਲੈ ਰਾਹੁ॥
Bhandho hovai dosatee bhandho chalai raaho

ਭੰਡੁ ਮੁਆ ਭੰਡੁ ਭਾਲੀਐ ਭੰਡਿ ਹੋਵੈ ਬੰਧਾਨੁ॥
Bhand muaa bhand bhalee-ai bhand hovai bandhaan

ਸੋ ਕਿਉ ਮੰਦਾ ਆਖੀਐ ਜਿਤੁ ਜੰਮਹਿ ਰਾਜਾਨ॥
So kio mandaa aakhee-ai jit jammeh raajaan

ਭੰਡਹੁ ਹੀ ਭੰਡੁ ਉਪਜੈ ਭੰਡੈ ਬਾਝੁ ਨ ਕੋਇ॥
Bhandho hee bhand oopajai bhandai baajh na ko-ei

ਨਾਨਕ ਭੰਡੈ ਬਾਹਰਾ ਏਕੋ ਸਚਾ ਸੋਇ॥
Naanak bhandai baahraa ayko sachaa so-ei

ਜਿਤੁ ਮੁਖਿ ਸਦਾ ਸਾਲਾਹੀਐ ਭਾਗਾ ਰਤੀ ਚਾਰਿ
Jit mukh sadaa saalaahee-ai bhaagaa ratee chaar

ਨਾਨਕ ਤੇ ਮੁਖ ਉਜਲੇ ਤਿਤੁ ਸਚੈ ਦਰਬਾਰਿ॥
Naanak tay mukh oojalay tit sachai darbaar

From woman, man is born; within woman, man is conceived;
to woman he is engaged and married.

Woman becomes his friend; through woman,
the future generations come.

When his woman dies, he seeks another woman;
to woman he is bound.

So why call her bad? From her, kings are born.

From woman, woman is born;
without woman, there would be no one at all.

O Nanak, only the True Lord is without a woman.

That mouth which praises the Lord continually is
blessed and beautiful.

O Nanak, those faces shall be radiant in
the Court of the True Lord.

Divine Mother: In praise of the universal mother, the creative
power of woman, and in honor of woman's true divine nature.

This mantra is attributed to *Guru Nanak in the Siri Guru
Granth Sahib*. Highly controversial in his day, Guru Nanak
Dev Ji stood against the tyranny, abuse, and disrespect of
women that exists in society. He is often called the first
emancipator of women.

Pootaa Maataa Kee Aasees

Guru Arjan Dev Ji
Raag Gujri
496

ਜਿਸੁ ਸਿਮਰਤ ਸਭਿ ਕਿਲਵਿਖ ਨਾਸਹਿ ਪਿਤਰੀ ਹੋਇ ਉਧਾਰੋ॥
Jis simarat sabh kilvikh naaseh pitaree ho-ei udhaaro.

ਸੋ ਹਰਿ ਹਰਿ ਤੁਮ ਸਦ ਹੀ ਜਾਪਹੁ ਜਾ ਕਾ ਅੰਤੁ ਨ ਪਾਰੋ॥
So har har tum sad hee jaapaho jaa kaa ant na paaro

ਪੂਤਾ ਮਾਤਾ ਕੀ ਆਸੀਸ॥
Pootaa maataa kee aasees

ਨਿਮਖ ਨ ਬਿਸਰਉ ਤੁਮ ਕਉ ਹਰਿ ਹਰਿ ਸਦਾ ਭਜਹੁ ਜਗਦੀਸ॥ ਰਹਾਉ॥
Nimakh na bisarao tum kao har har sadaa bhajho jagdees || Rahaao

ਸਤਿਗੁਰੁ ਤੁਮ ਕਉ ਹੋਇ ਦਇਆਲਾ ਸੰਤਸੰਗਿ ਤੇਰੀ ਪ੍ਰੀਤਿ॥
Satgur tum kao ho-ei deiaalaa santsang tayree preet

ਕਾਪੜੁ ਪਤਿ ਪਰਮੇਸਰੁ ਰਾਖੀ ਭੋਜਨੁ ਕੀਰਤਨੁ ਨੀਤਿ॥
Kaapar pat paramaysar raakhee bhojan keertan neet

ਅੰਮ੍ਰਿਤੁ ਪੀਵਹੁ ਸਦਾ ਚਿਰੁ ਜੀਵਹੁ ਹਰਿ ਸਿਮਰਤ ਅਨਦ ਅਨੰਤਾ॥
Amrit peevho sadaa chir jeevho har simarat anad anantaa

ਰੰਗ ਤਮਾਸਾ ਪੂਰਨ ਆਸਾ ਕਬਹਿ ਨ ਬਿਆਪੈ ਚਿੰਤਾ॥
Rang tamaasaa pooran aasaa kabeh na biaapai chintaa

ਭਵਰੁ ਤੁਮ੍ਹਾਰਾ ਇਹੁ ਮਨੁ ਹੋਵਉ ਹਰਿ ਚਰਨਾ ਹੋਹੁ ਕਉਲਾ॥
Bhavar tamaaraa eiho man hovao har charnaa hohu kaolaa

ਨਾਨਕ ਦਾਸੁ ਓਨ ਸੰਗਿ ਲਪਟਾਇਓ ਜਿਉ ਬੂੰਦਹਿ ਚਾਤ੍ਰਿਕੁ ਮਉਲਾ॥
Naanak daas on sang laptaa-ei-o jio boondeh chaatrik maolaa

Remembering God, all mistakes are erased and
one's ancestors are redeemed and saved.

Always chant God's Name, Har, Har.
God is inside you, God is infinite.

O my child, this is your mother's blessing,

May you never forget God, Har, Har even for a moment,
worshipping forever the Lord of the Universe.

May the True Guru be kind to you;
may you love to be in the society of the Saints.

May your clothing be the protection of God;
may your food be the singing of God's praise.

Drink the nectar of God's Name and may you live long;
may meditation on God bring you endless bliss.

May joy and pleasure be yours and your hopes fulfilled;
may you never be worn by worry.

Let this mind of yours be the bumble bee,
and let the Lord's feet be the Lotus flower.

O Servant Nanak, link your mind in this way.
Like the sparrow hawk finding a raindrop, blossom forth.

From the *Siri Guru Granth Sahib*, Guru Arjan Dev Ji.

Divine Mother: This is a blessing from the mother that her child may ever feel Divine.

This shabad is from the Siri Guru Granth Sahib, and was written by Guru Arjan Dev Ji. Yogi Bhajan taught mothers to repeat this prayer for their child's protection and blessing. Some mothers say it daily, and some repeat it 11, 54, or 108 times on their child's birthday. Yogi Bhajan spoke of it once during a lecture at Khalsa Women's Training Camp in New Mexico in 1977. He said, "Jesus asked Mary if Joseph was his father. She told Jesus, 'Your father lives in the heavens.' This Jesus wanted to know, and knew when he was so little. During the entire life of that individual, the Heavenly Father was his father. Who was Mary? She was a very Divine mother who could create her son to be a Christ, who was pure."

Yogi Bhajan thus encouraged all mothers to see the Divine in our children and teach them to relate to it every day.

Elevation

Aad Sach Jugaad Sach

Guru Nanak Dev Ji
Japji Sahib
1

ਆਦਿ ਸਚੁ ਜੁਗਾਦਿ ਸਚੁ॥ਹੈ ਭੀ ਸਚੁ ਨਾਨਕ ਹੋਸੀ ਭੀ ਸਚੁ॥
Aad Sach Jugaad Sach Hai *Bhee Sach* Naanak Hosee *Bhee* Sach

or

Guru Arjan Dev Ji
Raag Gauree
285

ਆਦਿ ਸਚੁ ਜੁਗਾਦਿ ਸਚੁ॥ਹੈ ਭਿ ਸਚੁ ਨਾਨਕ ਹੋਸੀ ਭਿ ਸਚੁ॥
Aad Sach Jugaad Sach Hai *Bhei* Sach Naanak Hosee *Bhei* Sach

True in the beginning, true throughout the ages,
true even now, Nanak, truth shall ever be.

True in the beginning, true throughout the ages,
true even now, Nanak, truth shall ever be.

Elevation: To leverage yourself out of being stuck.

The 'Bhee' version of this mantra has essentially the same meaning and impact as the 'Bhei' version; however, the focus of the Bhei version is to remove blocks when you are stuck and get you moving. When Guru Arjan Dev Ji, the Fifth Guru of the Sikhs, was composing *Sukhmanee Sahib*, the great Sikh prayer of perfect peace, he came to an impass after completing sixteen *astpadis*, or verses. Baba Siri Chand, the elder son of Guru Nanak Dev Ji and founder of the Udasi order, met Guru Arjan Dev Ji at that time and was asked by the Guru to continue the composition. In humility, Baba Siri Chand only recited the slok of Guru Nanak Dev Ji at the end of the Mool Mantra: Aad Sach, Jugaad Sach; Hai Bhei Sach, Nanak Hosee Bhai Sach, only changing bhee to bhei, which removes blocks. This slok was thereupon repeated by Guru Arjan Dev Ji and set at the beginning of the seventeenth astpadi.

Ajai Alai

ਅਜੈ ॥ ਅਲੈ ॥ ਅਭੈ ॥ ਅਬੈ ॥
Ajai, Alai, Abhai, Abai

ਅਭੂ ॥ ਅਜੂ ॥ ਅਨਾਸ ॥ ਅਕਾਸ ॥
Abhoo, Ajoo, Anaas, Akaas

ਅਗੰਜ ॥ ਅਭੰਜ ॥ ਅਲੱਖ ॥ ਅਭੱਖ ॥
Aganj, Abhanj, Alakkh, Abhakkh

ਅਕਾਲ ॥ ਦਿਆਲ ॥ ਅਲੇਖ ॥ ਅਭੇਖ ॥
Akaal, Dyaal, Alaykh, Abhaykh

ਅਨਾਮ ॥ ਅਕਾਮ ॥ ਅਗਾਹ ॥ ਅਢਾਹ ॥
Anaam, Akaam, Agaa-eh, Adhaa-eh

ਅਨਾਥੇ ॥ ਪ੍ਰਮਾਥੇ ॥ ਅਜੋਨੀ ॥ ਅਮੋਨੀ ॥
Anaathay, Pramaathay, Ajonee, Amonee

ਨ ਰਾਗੇ ॥ ਨ ਰੰਗੇ ॥ ਨ ਰੂਪੇ ॥ ਨ ਰੇਖੇ ॥
Na Raagay, Na Rangay, Na Roopay, Na Raykhay

ਅਕਰਮੰ ॥ ਅਭਰਮੰ ॥ ਅਗੰਜੇ ॥ ਅਲੇਖੇ ॥
Akarmang, Abharmang, Aganjay, Alaykhay

Invincible, Indestructible, Fearless, Unchanging

Unformed, Unborn, Imperishable, Etheric

Unbreakable, Impenetrable, Unseen, Unaffected

Undying, Merciful, Indescribable, Uncostumed

Nameless, Desireless, Unfathomable, Incorruptible

Unmastered, Destroyer, Beyond birth, Beyond silence

Beyond love, Beyond color, Beyond form, Beyond shape

Beyond karma, Beyond doubt, Unconquerable, Indescribable

Elevation: Lifts one from depression and anger.

Whenever you are in trouble mentally or you are being mentally attacked in one way or another, chant these words and opposition will dissolve before you.

From the *Siri Guru Granth Sahib*, Dasam Granth, Jaap Sahib, Guru Gobind Singh pages 189-196

Anand Bhei-aa Mayree Maa-ay

Guru Amar Daas Ji
Anand Sahib

ਅਨੰਦੁ ਭਇਆ ਮੇਰੀ ਮਾਏ
Anand bhei-aa mayree maa-ay

ਸਤਿਗੁਰੁ ਮੈ ਪਾਇਆ ॥
Sat Guroo mai paaei-aa

O my mother, I am in ecstasy

By the grace of the true Guru.

Elevation: Releases one from suffering and sorrow and uplifts the human spirit.

From the *Siri Guru Granth Sahib*, Guru Amar Daas Ji Raag Raamkalee, page 917

Chakkar Chihan

Guru Gobind Singh
Dasam Granth
Jaap Sahib page 2

ਚੱਕ੍ਰ ਚਿਹਨ ਅਰੁ ਬਰਨ ਜਾਤਿ ਅਰੁ ਪਾਤਿ ਨਹਿਨ ਜਿਹ॥
Chakkar chihan ar baran Jaat ar paat nahin jeh

ਰੂਪ ਰੰਗ ਅਰੁ ਰੇਖ ਭੇਖ ਕੋਊ ਕਹਿ ਨ ਸਕਤਿ ਕਿਹ॥
Roop rang ar raykh bhayk ko-oo kaeh na sakat keh

ਅਚਲ ਮੂਰਤਿ ਅਨਭਉ ਪ੍ਰਕਾਸ ਅਮਿਤੋਜਿ ਕਹਿੱਜੈ॥
Achal moorat anbhau prakaas amitoj kahijai

ਕੋਟਿ ਇੰਦੂ ਇੰਦੁਾਨਿ ਸਾਹੁ ਸਾਹਾਨਿ ਗਨਿੱਜੈ॥
Kot indr indraan shaa-eh shaahaan ganijai

ਤ੍ਰਿਭਵਣ ਮਹੀਪ ਸੁਰ ਨਰ ਅਸੁਰ ਨੇਤ ਨੇਤ ਬਨ ਤ੍ਰਿਣ ਕਹਤ॥
Tribhavan maheep sur nar asur nayt nayt ban trin kahat

ਤਵ ਸਰਬ ਨਾਮ ਕਥੈ ਕਵਨ ਕਰਮ ਨਾਮ ਬਰਨਤ ਸੁਮਤਿ॥
Tva sarab naam kathai kavan karam naam barnat sumat

O Lord, You are such a Being who has no physical appearance,
such as form, color, shape, marks, symbols, and garb.

You do not belong to any caste, class, or lineage.

You are immutable (unchanging), self-luminous, and shine
everywhere in Your splendor. You have limitless powers.

You are the maker of billions of kings like Indra.

You are the King of kings.

You are the Master of all the three spheres.

Besides gods, humans, and demons, even all the
vegetative creation in the woodlands say:
You are Infinite, You are Infinite.
Who can describe all Your Names?

The wise men have mentioned only the names of Your actions.

Elevation: Uplifts your heart and mind to experience the love of your soul.

Cheet Aavai Taa Mahaa Anand

Guru Arjan Dev Ji
Raag Bhairao
1141

ਚੀਤਿ ਆਵੈ ਤਾਂ ਮਹਾ ਅਨੰਦ॥
Cheet aavai taa mahaa anand

ਚੀਤਿ ਆਵੈ ਤਾਂ ਸਭਿ ਦੁਖ ਭੰਜ॥
Cheet aavai taa sabh dukh bhanj

ਚੀਤਿ ਆਵੈ ਤਾਂ ਸਰਧਾ ਪੂਰੀ॥
Cheet aavai taa sardhaa pooree

ਚੀਤਿ ਆਵੈ ਤਾਂ ਕਬਹਿ ਨ ਝੂਰੀ॥
Cheet aavai taa kabeh na jhooree

ਅੰਤਰਿ ਰਾਮ ਰਾਇ ਪ੍ਰਗਟੇ ਆਇ॥
Antar raam raa-ei pargatay aa-ei

ਗੁਰਿ ਪੂਰੈ ਦੀਓ ਰੰਗੁ ਲਾਇ॥ 1 ॥ ਰਹਾਉ॥
Gur poorai deeo rang laa-ei || Rahaao

ਚੀਤਿ ਆਵੈ ਤਾਂ ਸਰਬ ਕੋ ਰਾਜਾ॥
Cheet aavai taa sarab ko raajaa

ਚੀਤਿ ਆਵੈ ਤਾਂ ਪੂਰੇ ਕਾਜਾ॥
Cheet aavai taa pooray kaajaa

ਚੀਤਿ ਆਵੈ ਤਾਂ ਰੰਗਿ ਗੁਲਾਲ॥
Cheet aavai taa rang gulaal

ਚੀਤਿ ਆਵੈ ਤਾਂ ਸਦਾ ਨਿਹਾਲ॥
Cheet aavai taa sadaa nihaal

ਚੀਤਿ ਆਵੈ ਤਾਂ ਸਦ ਧਨਵੰਤਾ॥
Cheet aavai taa sad dhanvantaa

ਚੀਤਿ ਆਵੈ ਤਾਂ ਸਦ ਨਿਭਰੰਤਾ॥
Cheet aavai taa sad nibhrantaa

ਚੀਤਿ ਆਵੈ ਤਾਂ ਸਭਿ ਰੰਗ ਮਾਣੇ॥
Cheet aavai taa sabh rang maanay

ਚੀਤਿ ਆਵੈ ਤਾਂ ਚੂਕੀ ਕਾਣੇ॥
Cheet aavai taa chukee kaanay

ਚੀਤਿ ਆਵੈ ਤਾਂ ਸਹਜ ਘਰੁ ਪਾਇਆ॥
Cheet aavai taa sahej ghar paaei-aa

ਚੀਤਿ ਆਵੈ ਤਾਂ ਸੁੰਨਿ ਸਮਾਇਆ॥
Cheet aavai taa sunn samaaei-aa

ਚੀਤਿ ਆਵੈ ਸਦ ਕੀਰਤਨੁ ਕਰਤਾ ॥

Cheet aavai sad keertan kartaa

ਮਨੁ ਮਾਨਿਆ ਨਾਨਕ ਭਗਵੰਤਾ ॥

Man maaniaa Naanak bhagvantaa

When He comes to mind,
then I am in supreme bliss.

When He comes to mind,
then all my pains are shattered.

When He comes to mind,
my hopes are fulfilled.

When He comes to mind,
I never feel sadness.

Deep within my being,
my Sovereign Lord King has
revealed Himself to me.

The Perfect Guru has inspired me
to love Him. Pause

When He comes to mind,
I am the king of all.

When He comes to mind,
all my affairs are completed.

When He comes to mind,
I am dyed in the deep crimson of His Love.

When He comes to mind,
I am ecstatic forever.

When He comes to mind,
I am wealthy forever.

When He comes to mind,
I am free of doubt forever.

When He comes to mind,
then I enjoy all pleasures.

When He comes to mind,
I am rid of fear.

When He comes to mind,
I find the home of peace and poise.

When He comes to mind,
I am absorbed in the Primal Void of God.

When He comes to mind,
I continually sing the Kirtan of His Praises.

Nanak's mind is pleased and
satisfied with the Lord God.

From the *Siri Guru Granth Sahib*, Guru Arjun Dev Ji, pg 1141.

Elevation: Takes away suffering and pain.

Har Har Whaa-hay Guroo

ਹਰਿ ਹਰਿ ਵਾਹਿਗੁਰੂ
Har Har Whaa-hay Guroo

The Creator is bliss;
great is the Guru.

Elevation: Removes phobias and subconscious blocks from the past.

This mantra creates balance between earth and ether and restores equilibrium, so past karmas are cleared.

Jis No Bakhshay

Guru Nanak Dev Ji
Japji Sahib
Siri Guru Granth Sahib page 5

ਜਿਸ ਨੋ ਬਖਸੇ ਸਿਫਤਿ ਸਾਲਾਹ ॥
Jis no bakhshay sifat saalaah

ਨਾਨਕ ਪਾਤਿਸਾਹੀ ਪਾਤਿਸਾਹੁ ॥
Naanak paatishaahee paatishaaho

One who is blessed to sing the Praises of the Divine Master,

O Nanak, is the King of kings.

Elevation: To get out of depression.

From *Japji Sahib*, page 5.

Mai Andhulay Kee Tayk

Bhagat Naam Dev Ji
Raag Tilang
727

ਮੈ ਅੰਧੁਲੇ ਕੀ ਟੇਕ ਤੇਰਾ ਨਾਮੁ ਖੁੰਦਕਾਰਾ॥

Mai andhulay kee tayk tayraa naam khundkaaraa

ਮੈ ਗਰੀਬ ਮੈ ਮਸਕੀਨ ਤੇਰਾ ਨਾਮੁ ਹੈ ਅਧਾਰਾ॥ 1॥ ਰਹਾਉ॥

Mai gareeb mai maskeen tayraa naam hai adhaaraa. Rahaao

ਕਰੀਮਾਂ ਰਹੀਮਾਂ ਅਲਾਹ ਤੂ ਗਨੀ॥

Kareemaa raheemaa alaah too ganee

ਹਾਜਰਾ ਹਜੂਰਿ ਦਰਿ ਪੇਸਿ ਤੂੰ ਮਨੀ॥

Haajraa hajoor dar pays toon manee

ਦਰੀਆਉ ਤੂ ਦਿਹੰਦ ਤੂ ਬਿਸੀਆਰ ਤੂ ਧਨੀ॥

Dareeaa-ou too dihand too bisee-aar too dhanee

ਦੇਹਿ ਲੇਹਿ ਏਕੁ ਤੂੰ ਦਿਗਰ ਕੋ ਨਹੀ॥

Dayeh layeh ayk too(n) digar ko nahee

ਤੂੰ ਦਾਨਾਂ ਤੂੰ ਬੀਨਾਂ ਮੈ ਬੀਚਾਰੁ ਕਿਆ ਕਰੀ॥

Too(n) daanaa too(n) beenaa mai beechaar kiaa karee

ਨਾਮੇ ਚੇ ਸੁਆਮੀ ਬਖਸੰਦ ਤੂੰ ਹਰੀ॥

Naamay chay suaamee bakhsand too(n) haree

I am blind;
Your Name is my only support, O Lord.

I am poor and meek;
Your Name is my only support.

O beautiful, benevolent and merciful Lord,
You are wealthy and generous.

You are ever present in every presence,
within me and before me.

O river of life and giver of all,
Your wealth is abundant.

You alone give, You alone take away,
You never falter.

O Wise One, O Supreme Seer,
You are beyond my comprehension.

O Lord and Master of Naam Dev,
You are ever forgiving and merciful.

Elevation: Brings clarity and the light of understanding.

Taken from the Siri Guru Granth Sahib, and written by
Bhagat Naam Dev Ji. When we are steeped in confusion
and doubt, this mantra lifts us out of the darkness and
brings clarity and the light of understanding.

Pavan Guroo Paanee Pitaa

Guru Nanak Dev Ji
Japji Sahib
Siri Guru Granth Sahib page 8

ਪਵਣੁ ਗੁਰੂ ਪਾਣੀ ਪਿਤਾ ਮਾਤਾ ਧਰਤਿ ਮਹਤੁ॥
Pavan guroo paanee pitaa maataa dharat mahat

ਦਿਵਸੁ ਰਾਤਿ ਦੁਇ ਦਾਈ ਦਾਇਆ ਖੇਲੈ ਸਗਲ ਜਗਤੁ॥
Divas raat du-ei daa-ee dhaa-ei-aa khaylai sagal jagat

ਚੰਗਿਆਈਆ ਬੁਰਿਆਈਆ ਵਾਚੈ ਧਰਮੁ ਹਦੂਰਿ॥
Changiaa-ee-aa buriaa-ee-aa vaachai dharam hadoor

ਕਰਮੀ ਆਪੋ ਆਪਣੀ ਕੇ ਨੇੜੈ ਕੇ ਦੂਰਿ॥
Karmee aapo aapanee kay nayrai kay door

ਜਿਨੀ ਨਾਮੁ ਧਿਆਇਆ ਗਏ ਮਸਕਤਿ ਘਾਲਿ॥
Jinee naam dhiaa-ei-aa ga-ay masakat ghaal

ਨਾਨਕ ਤੇ ਮੁਖ ਉਜਲੇ ਕੇਤੀ ਛੁਟੀ ਨਾਲਿ॥
Naanak tay mukh ujalay kaytee chhutee naal

The pranic wind is the Guru,

water is the Father,

and earth is the Great Mother of all.

Day and night are the two nurses,

in whose lap all the world is at play.

Good deeds and bad deeds —
the record is read out

in the presence of the Lord of Dharma.

According to their own actions,
some are drawn closer,
and some are driven farther away.

Those who have meditated on the Naam,
the Name of the Lord,

and departed after having worked by
the sweat of their brow,

O Nanak, their faces are radiant in
the Court of the Lord.

They are saved and many others are
saved along with them!

Elevation: Brings self-fulfillment, elevation,
acknowledgement and respect.

From the *Siri Guru Granth Sahib*, the slok following the 38th
pauree of Japji Sahib, by Guru Nanak.

Pritham Bhagautee

Guru Gobind Singh, Chandi di Vaar
Dasam Granth
page 278

Added lines from the Ardas.

ਪ੍ਰਿਥਮ ਭਗੌਤੀ ਸਿਮਰਿ ਕੈ ਗੁਰ ਨਾਨਕ ਲਈਂ ਧਿਆਇ॥
Pritham bhagautee simar kai Gur Naanak laee dhiaa-ei

ਫਿਰ ਅੰਗਦ ਗੁਰ ਤੇ ਅਮਰਦਾਸੁ ਰਾਮਦਾਸੈ ਹੋਈਂ ਸਹਾਇ॥
Fir Angad Gur tay Amar Daas Raam Daasai hoee sahaa-ei

ਅਰਜਨ ਹਰਗੋਬਿੰਦ ਨੋ ਸਿਮਰੌ ਸ੍ਰੀ ਹਰਿਰਾਇ॥
Arjan Hargobind no simarau Siree Har Raa-ei

ਸ੍ਰੀ ਹਰਿਕ੍ਰਿਸਨ ਧਿਆਈਐ ਜਿਸੁ ਡਿਠੈ ਸਭਿ ਦੁਖ ਜਾਇ॥
Siree Har Krishan dhiaa-ee-ai jis dithai sabh dukh jaa-ei

ਤੇਗ ਬਹਾਦਰ ਸਿਮਰਿਐ ਘਰ ਨਉ ਨਿਧਿ ਆਵੈ ਧਾਇ॥
Tayg Bahaadar simari-ai ghar nau nidh aavai dhaa-ei

ਸਭ ਥਾਈਂ ਹੋਇ ਸਹਾਇ॥
Sabh thaaee ho-ei sahaa-ei

ਦਸਵੇਂ ਪਾਤਿਸ਼ਾਹ ਸ੍ਰੀ ਗੁਰੂ ਗੋਬਿੰਦ ਸਿੰਘ ਸਾਹਿਬ ਜੀ ਸਭ ਥਾਈਂ ਹੋਇ ਸਹਾਇ॥

**Dasvay paatishah Siree Guroo Gobind Singh
Saahib Jee sabh thaa-ee ho-ei sahaa-ei**

ਧੰਨ ਧੰਨ ਸ੍ਰੀ ਗੁਰੂ ਗ੍ਰੰਥ ਸਾਹਿਬ ਜੀ ਦੇ ਪਾਠ ਦੀਦਾਰ ਦਾ
ਧਿਆਨ ਧਰ ਕੇ ਬੋਲੋ ਜੀ ਵਾਹਿਗੁਰੂ॥

**Dhan Dhan Siree Guroo Granth Saahib Jee day
Paath deedaar daa dhiaan dhar kay bolo jee Whaa-hay Guroo**

After first remembering the Adi Shakti,
the Primal Power,

Meditate on Guru Nanak,
then Guru Angad,

Guru Amar Das and Guru Ram Das,
the fountain of eternal peace.

Meditate on Guru Arjun, Guru Hargobind,
and Guru Har Rai.

Meditate on Siri Guru Har Krishan,
and all your sufferings shall vanish.

Meditate on Guru Tegh Bahadur,
and the nine treasures shall come running to you.

Great, great is the Tenth Master, Guru Gobind Singh,
through whom all places are in peace.

The light of the ten Gurus,
the Siri Guru Granth Sahib Ji,

Hail! Hail! the Siri Guru Granth Sahib,
the light of the ten Gurus,

Whose words are jewels of meditation.

Elevation: A prayer to set ourselves to walk in
the frequency of the Gurus throughout the day.

We recite Pritam Bhagautee at the beginning of
Ardas (Sikh prayer) each morning and at all times
when attending the Guru, or for individual prayers.

Sochai Soch Na Hova-ee

Guru Nanak Dev Ji
Japji Sahib
Siri Guru Granth Sahib page 1

ਸੋਚੈ ਸੋਚਿ ਨ ਹੋਵਈ ਜੇ ਸੋਚੀ ਲਖ ਵਾਰ॥
Sochai soch na hova-ee jay sochee lakh vaar

ਚੁਪੈ ਚੁਪਿ ਨ ਹੋਵਈ ਜੇ ਲਾਇ ਰਹਾ ਲਿਵ ਤਾਰ॥
Chupai chup na hova-ee jay laa-eh rahaa liv taar

ਭੁਖਿਆ ਭੁਖ ਨ ਉਤਰੀ ਜੇ ਬੰਨਾ ਪੁਰੀਆ ਭਾਰ॥
Bhukhiaa bhukh na utree jay bannaa puree-aa bhaar

ਸਹਸ ਸਿਆਣਪਾ ਲਖ ਹੋਹਿ ਤ ਇਕ ਨ ਚਲੈ ਨਾਲਿ॥
Sahas siaanpaa lakh hoeh ta eik na chalai naal

ਕਿਵ ਸਚਿਆਰਾ ਹੋਈਐ ਕਿਵ ਕੂੜੈ ਤੁਟੈ ਪਾਲਿ॥
Kiv sachiaaraa hoee-ai kiv koorai tutai paal

ਹੁਕਮਿ ਰਜਾਈ ਚਲਣਾ ਨਾਨਕ ਲਿਖਿਆ ਨਾਲਿ॥
Hukam rajaa-ee chalnaa Naanak likhiaa naal

By thinking and thinking again one
hundred thousand times one cannot find a solution.

By being quiet peace cannot be found,
even if poised in deep meditation forever.

The hunger of the hungry cannot be quenched
even if carrying heavy loads of food.

One may possess one hundred thousand clever ideas but
not even one will accompany you.

How can one be purified and the veil of illusion dispelled?

Oh Nanak, walk in Divine Will. It was so preordained.

Elevation: Lifts you from the deepest depression,
insecurity, nightmares, and loss.

From the *Siri Guru Granth Sahib*, 1st pauree of Japji Sahib,
by Guru Nanak. The total knowledge of God and ecstasy
is contained in this pauree. It is an antidote to depression.
When there is a tremendous, absolute temptation just
remember, thinking won't work, even if you think a hundred
thousand times. Remember, those who seek to learn from
time shall always be hung up in space. Because time creates
space. Timelessness is what you are.

Too(n) Mayraa Pitaa

Guru Arjan Dev Ji
Raag Maajh
103

ਤੂੰ ਮੇਰਾ ਪਿਤਾ ਤੂੰਹੈ ਮੇਰਾ ਮਾਤਾ॥

Too(n) mayraa pitaa too(n) hai mayraa maataa.

ਤੂੰ ਮੇਰਾ ਬੰਧਪੁ ਤੂੰ ਮੇਰਾ ਭ੍ਰਾਤਾ॥

Too(n) mayraa bandhap too(n) mayraa bhraataa

ਤੂੰ ਮੇਰਾ ਰਾਖਾ ਸਭਨੀ ਥਾਈ ਤਾ ਭਉ ਕੇਹਾ ਕਾੜਾ ਜੀਉ॥

Too(n) mayraa raakhaa sabhanee thaa-ee taa bhao kayhaa kaaraa jeeo

ਤੁਮਰੀ ਕ੍ਰਿਪਾ ਤੇ ਤੁਧੁ ਪਛਾਣਾ॥

Tumaree kirpaa tay tudh pachhaanaa

ਤੂੰ ਮੇਰੀ ਓਟ ਤੂੰਹੈ ਮੇਰਾ ਮਾਣਾ॥

Too(n) mayree ot too(n) hai mayraa maanaa

ਤੁਝ ਬਿਨੁ ਦੂਜਾ ਅਵਰੁ ਨ ਕੋਈ ਸਭੁ ਤੇਰਾ ਖੇਲੁ ਅਖਾੜਾ ਜੀਉ॥

Tujh bin dhoojaa avar na koee sabh
tayraa khayl akhaaraa jeeo

ਜੀਅ ਜੰਤ ਸਭਿ ਤੁਧੁ ਉਪਾਏ॥

Jeea jant sabh tudh upaa-ay

ਜਿਤੁ ਜਿਤੁ ਭਾਣਾ ਤਿਤੁ ਤਿਤੁ ਲਾਏ॥

Jit jit bhaanaa tit tit laa-ay

ਸਭ ਕਿਛੁ ਕੀਤਾ ਤੇਰਾ ਹੋਵੈ ਨਾਹੀ ਕਿਛੁ ਅਸਾੜਾ ਜੀਉ॥

Sabh kich keetaa tayraa hovai naahee kich asaarhaa jeeo

ਨਾਮੁ ਧਿਆਇ ਮਹਾ ਸੁਖੁ ਪਾਇਆ॥

Naam dheeaa-ei mahaa sukh paa-ei-aa

ਹਰਿ ਗੁਣ ਗਾਇ ਮੇਰਾ ਮਨੁ ਸੀਤਲਾਇਆ॥

Har gun gaa-ei mayraa man seetalaa-ei-aa

ਗੁਰਿ ਪੂਰੈ ਵਜੀ ਵਾਧਾਈ ਨਾਨਕ ਜਿਤਾ ਬਿਖਾੜਾ ਜੀਉ॥

Gur poorai vajee vaadhaa-ee Naanak jitaa bikhaaraa jeeo

You are my Father,
and You are my Mother.

You are my soul, my breath of life,
the Giver of Peace.

You are my Lord and Master;
I am Your slave.

Without You, I have no one at all.

Please bless me with Your mercy,
God, and give me this gift,

That I may sing Your praises,
day and night. Pause.

I am Your musical instrument,
and You are the Musician.

I am Your beggar;
please bless me with Your charity,
O Great Giver.

By Your Grace,
I enjoy love and pleasures.

You are deep within
each and every heart.

By Your Grace,
I chant the Name.

In the sadh sangat,
the company of the holy,
I sing Your glorious praises.

In Your mercy,
You take away our pains.

By Your mercy,
the heart lotus blossoms forth.

I am a sacrifice to the Divine Guru.

The blessed vision of Divine Darshan is
fruitful and rewarding;
The Master's service is
immaculate and pure.

Be Merciful to me,
O my Divine Master,

That Nanak may continually sing
your Glorious Praises.

Elevation: To become your own counselor.

Enlightenment

Giaan Khand Meh Giaan Parchand

Guru Nanak Dev Ji
Japji Sahib
7-8

ਗਿਆਨ ਖੰਡ ਮਹਿ ਗਿਆਨੁ ਪਰਚੰਡੁ॥
Giaan khand meh giaan parchand

ਤਿਥੈ ਨਾਦ ਬਿਨੋਦ ਕੋਡ ਅਨੰਦੁ॥
Tithai naad binod kod anand

ਸਰਮ ਖੰਡ ਕੀ ਬਾਣੀ ਰੂਪੁ॥
Saram khand kee baanee roop

ਤਿਥੈ ਘਾੜਤਿ ਘੜੀਐ ਬਹੁਤੁ ਅਨੂਪੁ॥
Tithai ghaarat gharee-ai bahut anoop

ਤਾ ਕੀਆ ਗਲਾ ਕਥੀਆ ਨਾ ਜਾਹਿ॥
Taa kee-aa galaa kathee-aa naa jaa-eh

ਜੇ ਕੋ ਕਹੈ ਪਿਛੈ ਪਛੁਤਾਇ॥
Jay ko kahai pichhai pachhutaa-ei

ਤਿਥੈ ਘੜੀਐ ਸੁਰਤਿ ਮਤਿ ਮਨਿ ਬੁਧਿ॥
Tithai gharee-ai surat mat man budh

ਤਿਥੈ ਘੜੀਐ ਸੁਰਾ ਸਿਧਾ ਕੀ ਸੁਧਿ॥
Tithai gharee-ai suraa sidhaa kee sudh

In the realm of wisdom,
spiritual wisdom reigns supreme.

There, the sound current of the Naad resounds
amid the sounds and sights of bliss.

In the realm of humility,
the Word is beauty.

There, forms of incomparable beauty
are fashioned.

These things cannot be described.

One who tries to speak of these
shall regret the attempt.

There, the intuition, intellect, mind,
and understanding are shaped.

There, the consciousness of
the spiritual warriors,

And the Siddhas, the beings of
spiritual perfection, are shaped.

From the Siri Guru Granth Sahib, the 36th pauree of Japji Sahib,
Guru Nanak Dev Ji.

Enlightenment: Brings divine realization and
understanding of the heavens and earth.

Mayraa Man Saadh Janaa Mil Hariaa

Guru Raam Daas Ji
Raag Kaanraa
1294

ਮੇਰਾ ਮਨੁ ਸਾਧ ਜਨਾਂ ਮਿਲਿ ਹਰਿਆ ॥

Mayraa man saadh janaa mil hariaa

ਹਉ ਬਲਿ ਬਲਿ ਬਲਿ ਬਲਿ ਸਾਧ ਜਨਾਂ ਕਉ ਮਿਲਿ
ਸੰਗਤਿ ਪਾਰਿ ਉਤਰਿਆ ॥ ਰਹਾਉ ॥

Hao bal bal bal bal saadh janaa kao
mil sangat paar utariaa. Rahaao

ਹਰਿ ਹਰਿ ਕ੍ਰਿਪਾ ਕਰਹੁ ਪ੍ਰਭ ਅਪਨੀ ਹਮ ਸਾਧ ਜਨਾਂ ਪਗ ਪਰਿਆ ॥

Har har kirpaa karaho prabh apanee ham saadh janaa pag pariaa

ਧਨੁ ਧਨੁ ਸਾਧ ਜਿਨ ਹਰਿ ਪ੍ਰਭੁ ਜਾਨਿਆ ਮਿਲਿ ਸਾਧੂ ਪਤਿਤ ਉਧਰਿਆ ॥

Dhan dhan saadh jin har prabh jaaniaa mil saadhoo patit udhariaa

ਮਨੂਆ ਚਲੈ ਚਲੈ ਬਹੁ ਬਹੁ ਬਿਧਿ ਮਿਲਿ ਸਾਧੂ ਵਸਗਤਿ ਕਰਿਆ ॥

Manuaa chalai chalai baho baho bidh mil saadhu vasgat kariaa

ਜਿਉਂ ਜਲ ਤੰਤੁ ਪਸਾਰਿਓ ਬਧਕਿ ਗ੍ਰਸਿ ਮੀਨਾ ਵਸਗਤਿ ਖਰਿਆ ॥

Jiu jal tant pasaario badhak garas meenaa vasgat khariaa

ਹਰਿ ਕੇ ਸੰਤ ਸੰਤ ਭਲ ਨੀਕੇ ਮਿਲਿ ਸੰਤ ਜਨਾ ਮਲੁ ਲਹੀਆ ॥

Har kay sant sant bhal neekay mil sant janaa mal lahiaa

ਹਉਮੈ ਦੁਰਤੁ ਗਇਆ ਸਭੁ ਨੀਕਰਿ ਜਿਉ ਸਾਬੁਨਿ ਕਾਪਰੁ ਕਰਿਆ ॥

Haumai durat gaei-aa sabh neekar jio saabun kaapar kariaa

ਮਸਤਕਿ ਲਿਲਾਟਿ ਲਿਖਿਆ ਧੁਰਿ ਠਾਕੁਰਿ ਗੁਰ ਸਤਿਗੁਰ ਚਰਨ ਉਰ ਧਰਿਆ ॥

Mastak lilaat likhiaa dhur thaakur gur satgur
charan ur dhariaa

ਸਭੁ ਦਾਲਦੁ ਦੂਖ ਭੰਜ ਪ੍ਰਭੁ ਪਾਇਆ ਜਨ ਨਾਨਕ ਨਾਮਿ ਉਧਰਿਆ ॥

Sabh daalad dookh bhanj prabh paaei-aa jan Naanak naam udhariaa

Meeting with the holy people, my mind blossoms forth.

I am a sacrifice, a sacrifice, a sacrifice, a sacrifice
unto those holy beings.

Joining the sangat, the holy congregation,
I am carried across to the other side. Pause.

O Lord, Har Har, please bless me with Your mercy,
that I may fall at the feet of the Holy.

Blessed, blessed are the Holy, who know the Lord God,
meeting with whom even sinners are saved.

The mind roams and rambles around in all directions.

Meeting with the Holy,
it is overpowered and brought under control.

Just as when the fisherman spreads his net over the water,
he catches and overpowers the fish.

The Saints, the Saints of the Lord are humble and good.

Meeting with the humble Saints, filth is washed away.

All the sins and egotism are washed away,
like soap washing dirty clothes.

According to that preordained destiny inscribed on
my forehead by my Lord and Master,

I have enshrined the feet of the Guru,
the true Guru, within my heart.

I have found God, the destroyer of all poverty and pain.

Servant Nanak is saved through the Naam.

From the *Siri Guru Granth Sahib, Guru Ram Das*, pg. 1274.

Enlightenment: Takes away neuroses and brings
the experience of realization and fulfillment
through the blessing of the Holy company.

Fulfillment

Apunay Sayvak Kee

Guru Arjan Dev Ji
Raag Aasaa
403

ਅਪੁਨੇ ਸੇਵਕ ਕੀ ਆਪੇ ਰਾਖੈ ਆਪੇ ਨਾਮੁ ਜਪਾਵੈ॥
Apunay sayvak kee aapay raakhai aapay naam japaavai.

He Himself preserves His servants;
He causes them to chant His Name.

Fulfillment: Develops inner strength, confidence,
and fulfillment.

Ardaas Bhaee

ਅਰਦਾਸ ਭਈ ਅਮਰਦਾਸ ਗੁਰੂ ਅਮਰਦਾਸ ਗੁਰੂ ਅਰਦਾਸ ਭਈ,
Ardaas Bhaee Amar Daas Guroo,
Amar Daas Guroo, Ardaas Bhaee

ਰਾਮਦਾਸ ਗੁਰੂ ਰਾਮਦਾਸ ਗੁਰੂ ਰਾਮਦਾਸ ਗੁਰੂ ਸਚੀ ਸਹੀ
Raam Daas Guroo, Raam Daas Guroo,
Raam Daas Guroo, Sachee Sahee

The prayer that has been made to Guru Amar Das
is guaranteed by Guru Ram Das. The miracle is complete.

Fulfillment: Life is adjusted according to your needs.

Ardas Bhaee is a prayer mantra. If you sing it,
your mind, body, and soul automatically combine,
and without even saying what you want, your life
is adjusted according to your needs. That is the
beauty and power of this prayer.

Guru Amar Das is the energy of grace and hope when there is no hope. Guru Ram Das is the energy of miracles, healings, and blessings. This is the mantra for prayers to be answered. *Guru* is that which directs one from (gu) darkness to (ru) light; from ignorance to the experience of one's infinite nature. Guru Amar Das is the third of the Sikh Gurus; he embodies generosity and equality. Guru Ram Das, his son-in-law, is the fourth of the Sikh Gurus; he embodies humility, loving service, and compassion. *Ram* means servant of all. Normally there is no power in the human but the power of prayer. And to do prayer, you have to put your mind and body together and then pray from the soul. Chanting this mantra does that for you.

Jat Paahaaraa Dheeraj Suniaar

Guru Nanak Dev Ji
Japji Sahib
8

ਜਤੁ ਪਾਹਾਰਾ ਧੀਰਜੁ ਸੁਨਿਆਰੁ॥
Jat paahaaraa dheeraj suniaar

ਅਹਰਣਿ ਮਤਿ ਵੇਦੁ ਹਥੀਆਰੁ॥
Aharan mat vayd hathee-aar

ਭਉ ਖਲਾ ਅਗਨਿ ਤਪ ਤਾਉ॥
Bhao khalaa agan tap taao

ਭਾਂਡਾ ਭਾਉ ਅੰਮ੍ਰਿਤੁ ਤਿਤੁ ਢਾਲਿ॥
Bhaandaa bhaao ammrit tit dhaal

ਘੜੀਐ ਸਬਦੁ ਸਚੀ ਟਕਸਾਲ॥
Gharee-ai shabad sachee taksaal

ਜਿਨ ਕਉ ਨਦਰਿ ਕਰਮੁ ਤਿਨ ਕਾਰ॥
Jin kao nadar karam tin kaar

ਨਾਨਕ ਨਦਰੀ ਨਦਰਿ ਨਿਹਾਲ॥
Naanak nadaree nadar nihaal

Let self-control be your furnace,
and patience your goldsmith.

Let understanding be your anvil,
and spiritual wisdom the tools.

With the fear of God as your bellows,

Fan the flames of the body's inner heat, the tapa.

In the crucible of love,
melt the Nectar of the Name and
mint the coin of the Shabad Guru.

Such is the labor of those upon whom
He has cast His glance of Grace.

O Nanak, the Merciful Lord,
by His Grace, uplifts and exalts them!

From the *Siri Guru Granth Sahib*, the 38th pauree of
Japji Sahib, Guru Nanak Dev Ji.

Fulfillment: Gives you the power to rewrite
your own destiny.

Healing

Karan Kaaran Samrath Hai

Guru Arjan Dev Ji
Raag Bilaaval
818

ਕਰਣ ਕਾਰਣ ਸਮਰਥੁ ਹੈ ਤਿਸੁ ਬਿਨੁ ਨਹੀ ਹੋਰੁ ॥
Karan kaaran samrath hai tis bin nahee hor

The All-Powerful Lord is the Cause of causes;
there is no other than Him.

Healing: Brings clarity of mind.

Raam Daas Guroo Har Sat Keeyo

Bhatt Nal
Sawayai Mehla 2
1400

ਰਾਮਦਾਸੁ ਗੁਰੂ ਹਰਿ ਸਤਿ ਕੀਜਉ
Raam Daas Guroo har sat keeyo

ਸਮਰਥ ਗੁਰੂ ਸਿਰਿ ਹਥੁ ਧਰਿਉ ॥
Samrath Guroo siri hath dharyo

Guru Ram Das recognized the Divine Master as True.

The All-Powerful Guru places His hand upon my head.

Healing: Creates mental clarity and balance.

Intuition

Gobinday Mukanday Udaaray Apaaray
Hareeang Kareeang Nirnaamay Akaamay
Har Har Har Har

Guru Gobind Singh
Jaap Sahib

ਗੋਬਿੰਦੇ ॥ ਮੁਕੰਦੇ ॥ ਉਦਾਰੇ ॥ ਅਪਾਰੇ ॥
Gobinday, Mukanday, Udaaray, Apaaray

ਹਰੀਅੰ ॥ ਕਰੀਅੰ ॥ ਨ੍ਰਿਨਾਮੇ ॥ ਅਕਾਮੇ ॥
Hareeang, Kareeang, Nirnaamay, Akaamay

ਹਰ ਹਰ ਹਰ ਹਰ
Har Har Har Har

Sustainer, Liberator, Enlightener, Infinite

Destroyer, Creator, Nameless, Desireless

Infinite Creator, Infinite Creator
Infinite Creator, Infinite Creator

Intuition: Clears subconscious blocks and rebuilds self-esteem, while stimulating your sacred, intuitive mind.

The vibration of Har stimulates the meridians on the roof of the mouth to synchronize the hypothalamus and the pituitary gland, creating a functional intuitive mind. In addition, this mantra helps cleanse the subconscious mind, and balances the hemispheres of the brain, bringing compassion and patience.

Gobind Daas Tuhaar

Guru Gobind Singh
Amrit Keertan
838

ਸਗਲ ਦੁਆਰ ਕਉ ਛਾਡਿ ਕੈ ਗਹਿਓ ਤੁਹਾਰੋ ਦੁਆਰ॥
Sagal duaar kou chhaad kai gahi-ou tuhaaro duaar

ਬਾਂਹਿ ਗਹੇ ਕੀ ਲਾਜ ਅਸ ਗੋਬਿੰਦ ਦਾਸ ਤੁਹਾਰ॥
Baa-eh gahay kee laaj as Gobind daas tuhaar

Ignoring all others, I have taken refuge in You.

Oh Lord, only to You do I belong. Grant me Your protection.

Intuition: To develop trust in your intuitive mind.

Sach Khand Vasai Nirankaar

Guru Nanak Dev Ji
Japji Sahib
8

ਸਚ ਖੰਡਿ ਵਸੈ ਨਿਰੰਕਾਰੁ॥
Sach khand vasai nirankaar

ਕਰਿ ਕਰਿ ਵੇਖੈ ਨਦਰਿ ਨਿਹਾਲ॥
Kar kar vaykhai nadar nihaal

In the realm of Truth, the Formless Lord abides.

Having created the creation, He watches over it.
By His Glance of Grace, He bestows happiness.

Intuition: Awakens your intuitive mind to see beyond the veil of illusion.

Saa Taa Naa Maa –
Kirtan Kriya – The Panj Shabad

ਸਾ ਤਾ ਨਾ ਮਾ

Saa Taa Naa Maa

Saa – Infinity, totality of the cosmos

Taa – Existence, life, the birth of form from the Infinite

Naa – Death, or transformation

Maa – Rebirth

While chanting, touch the thumb to each of the four fingers in turn. In this way, we stimulate neural pathways to specific regions in the brain, which correspond to the planetary energies in the macrocosm of our solar system:

Saa – Index finger to thumb, Jupiter stimulates wisdom.

Taa – Middle finger to thumb, Saturn stimulates discipline, patience.

Naa – Ring finger to thumb, Sun stimulates health, radiance.

Maa – Little finger to thumb, Mercury stimulates communication.

Intuition: Increases intuition, balances the hemispheres of the brain and creates a destiny for someone who was not at all connected to his or her destiny.

This mantra is the atomic or Naad form of the mantra, *Sat Naam*. It is a great catalyst for change as it vibrates the continuous cycle of life and creation. The syllables *Sa Ta Na Ma* represent the five primal sounds of the universe. The fifth sound is "a," which is common to the other four, and together they cover the complete cycle of life (see page 7). This mantra is also known as Kirtan Kriya and the Panj Shabad. *Panj* means five.

Satnaam Satnaam Satnaam Jee

ਸਤਿਨਾਮ ਸਤਿਨਾਮ ਸਤਿਨਾਮ ਜੀ ਵਾਹਿਗੁਰੂ ਵਾਹਿਗੁਰੂ ਵਾਹਿਗੁਰੂ ਜੀ
Satnaam satnaam satnaam jee
Whaa-hay Guroo Whaa-hay Guroo Whaa-hay Guroo jee

Truth is the identity of my soul.
I dwell in the light of Divine wisdom and bliss.

Intuition: To speak clearly from the intuitive mind.

Karmic Clearing

Aakhan Jor

Guru Nanak Dev Ji
Japji Sahib
7

ਆਖਣਿ ਜੋਰੁ ਚੁਪੈ ਨਹ ਜੋਰੁ॥
Aakhan jor, chupai nah jor

ਜੋਰੁ ਨ ਮੰਗਣਿ ਦੇਣਿ ਨ ਜੋਰੁ॥
Jor na mangan dayn na jor

ਜੋਰੁ ਨ ਜੀਵਣਿ ਮਰਣਿ ਨਹ ਜੋਰੁ॥
Jor na jeevan maran nah jor

ਜੋਰੁ ਨ ਰਾਜਿ ਮਾਲਿ ਮਨਿ ਸੋਰੁ॥
Jor na raaj maal man sor

ਜੋਰੁ ਨ ਸੁਰਤੀ ਗਿਆਨਿ ਵੀਚਾਰਿ॥
Jor na surtee giaan veechaar

ਜੋਰੁ ਨ ਜੁਗਤੀ ਛੁਟੈ ਸੰਸਾਰੁ॥
Jor na jugatee chhutai sansaar

ਜਿਸੁ ਹਥਿ ਜੋਰੁ ਕਰਿ ਵੇਖੈ ਸੋਇ॥
Jis hath jor kar vaykhai so-ei

ਨਾਨਕ ਉਤਮੁ ਨੀਚੁ ਨ ਕੋਇ॥
Naanak utam neech na ko-ei

No power to speak, no power to keep silent.

No power to beg, no power to give.

No power to live, no power to die.

No power to rule, with wealth and occult mental powers.

No power to gain intuitive understanding,
to contemplate spiritual wisdom.

No power to find the way to escape from the world.

He alone has the power in His hands, He watches over all.

O Nanak, no one is high or low.

Clears Karma: Removes negativity and prevents
harm to others by your hand.

From the *Siri Guru Granth Sahib*, the 33rd pauree of
Japji Sahib, Guru Nanak Dev Ji.

This pauree destroys your ego and brings you
home to your divinity. It removes negativity and
neutralizes your destructive patterns.

Asee Khatay Bahut Kamaavday

Guru Amar Daas Ji
Salok Vaaraan Thay Vadheek
1416

ਅਸੀ ਖਤੇ ਬਹੁਤੁ ਕਮਾਵਦੇ ਅੰਤੁ ਨ ਪਾਰਾਵਾਰੁ॥
Asee khatay bahut kamaavday ant na paaraavaar

ਹਰਿ ਕਿਰਪਾ ਕਰਿ ਕੈ ਬਖਸਿ ਲੈਹੁ ਹਉ ਪਾਪੀ ਵਡ ਗੁਨਹਗਾਰੁ॥
Har kirpaa kar kai bakhas laiho hao paapee vad gunhagaar

I made so many mistakes; there is no end or limit to them.

O Master, You are merciful and forgive my offences.

Clears Karma: To acknowledge mistakes and adjust your course going forward.

Bharee-ai Hath Pair Tan Dayh

Guru Nanak Dev Ji
Japji Sahib
4

ਭਰੀਐ ਹਥੁ ਪੈਰੁ ਤਨੁ ਦੇਹ॥
Bharee-ai hath pair tan dayh

ਪਾਣੀ ਧੋਤੈ ਉਤਰਸੁ ਖੇਹ॥
Paanee dhotai utras khayh

ਮੂਤ ਪਲੀਤੀ ਕਪੜੁ ਹੋਇ॥
Moot paleetee kapar ho-ei

ਦੇ ਸਾਬੂਣੁ ਲਈਐ ਓਹੁ ਧੋਇ॥
Day saaboon laee-ai oho dho-ei

ਭਰੀਐ ਮਤਿ ਪਾਪਾ ਕੈ ਸੰਗਿ॥
Bharee-ai mat paapaa kai sang

ਓਹੁ ਧੋਪੈ ਨਾਵੈ ਕੈ ਰੰਗਿ॥
Oho dhopai naavai kai rang

ਪੁੰਨੀ ਪਾਪੀ ਆਖਣੁ ਨਾਹਿ ॥
Punee paapee aakhan naa-eh

ਕਰਿ ਕਰਿ ਕਰਣਾ ਲਿਖਿ ਲੈ ਜਾਹੁ ॥
Kar kar karnaa likh lai jaaho

ਆਪੇ ਬੀਜਿ ਆਪੇ ਹੀ ਖਾਹੁ ॥
Aapay beej aapay hee khaaho

ਨਾਨਕ ਹੁਕਮੀ ਆਵਹੁ ਜਾਹੁ ॥
Naanak hukamee aavaho jaaho

When the hands and body are covered with dirt,

water can wash them clean.

When the clothes are dirty and smeared with soil,

soap can remove the stain.

But when the mind is polluted by error and shame,

it can only be cleansed by the love of the Name.

When one is drawn by the virtuous or the vicious,

that also determines what is attracted to that one.

As you sow, so shall you reap.

O Nanak, by the Lord's command,

a person comes and goes in the cycle of life.

Clears Karma: Wipes away the karma of your past deeds.

This mantra is from the *Siri Guru Granth Sahib*, the 20th pauree of Japji Sahib, by Guru Nanak. It cleanses your soul. When monsters are nipping at your heels, the 20th pauree of Japji Sahib wipes your slate clean. This mantra takes away your false identity and brings realization of your Divine nature.

Gur Tuthai Har Prabh Mayliaa

Guru Amar Daas Ji
Salok Vaaraan Thay Vadheek
1416

ਗੁਰ ਤੁਠੈ ਹਰਿ ਪ੍ਰਭੁ ਮੇਲਿਆ ਸਭ ਕਿਲਵਿਖ ਕਟਿ ਵਿਕਾਰ॥

Gur tuthai har prabh mayliaa sabh kilvikh kat vikaar

The Guru's pleasure unites me with my Divine Master;
the Guru cuts away my past errors.

Clears Karma: Acceptance of Divine redemption.

Hamree Ganat Na Ganee-aa

Guru Arjan Dev Ji
Raag Sorath
619

ਹਮਰੀ ਗਣਤ ਨ ਗਣੀਆ ਕਾਈ ਅਪਨਾ ਬਿਰਦੁ ਪਛਾਨਿ॥

Hamree ganat na ganee-aa kaa-ee apnaa birad pachhaan.

He did not take my accounts into account;
such is His forgiving nature.

Clears Karma: For personal blessings to move
forward when you feel blocked.

Har Joo Raakh Layho Pat Mayree

Guru Tegh Bahaadur Ji
Raag Jaithsree
703

ਹਰਿ ਜੂ ਰਾਖਿ ਲੇਹੁ ਪਤਿ ਮੇਰੀ॥

Har joo raakh layho pat mayree.

O Dear Lord, please, save my honor!

Clears Karma: Brings self-forgiveness and
protection from past karma.

Eik Doo Jeebhau Lakh Ho-eh

Guru Nanak Dev Ji
Japji Sahib
7

ਇਕ ਦੂ ਜੀਭੌ ਲਖ ਹੋਹਿ ਲਖ ਹੋਵਹਿ ਲਖ ਵੀਸ॥
Eik doo jeebhau lakh ho-eh lakh hoveh lakh vees

ਲਖੁ ਲਖੁ ਗੇੜਾ ਆਖੀਅਹਿ ਏਕੁ ਨਾਮੁ ਜਗਦੀਸ॥
Lakh lakh gayraa aakhee-eh ayk naam jagdees

ਏਤੁ ਰਾਹਿ ਪਤਿ ਪਵੜੀਆ ਚੜੀਐ ਹੋਇ ਇਕੀਸ॥
Ayt raa-eh pat pavaree-aa charee-ai ho-ei eikees

ਸੁਣਿ ਗਲਾ ਆਕਾਸ ਕੀ ਕੀਟਾ ਆਈ ਰੀਸ॥
Sun galaa aakaas kee keetaa aa-ee rees

ਨਾਨਕ ਨਦਰੀ ਪਾਈਐ ਕੂੜੀ ਕੂੜੈ ਠੀਸ॥
Naanak nadaree paaee-ai kooree koorai thees

If I had one hundred thousand tongues,
and these were multiplied twenty times more,

with each tongue I would repeat,

hundreds of thousands of times,
the Name of the One,

the Lord of the universe.

Along this path to our Husband Lord,

We climb the steps of the ladder,
and come to merge with Him.

Hearing of the etheric realms,
even worms long to come back home.

O Nanak, by His Grace, He is obtained.

False are the boastings of the false.

This mantra comes from the *Siri Guru Granth Sahib*,
the 32nd pauree of Japji Sahib, by Guru Nanak.

Clears Karma: Pays your debts and completes
your karma.

Jagat Jalandaa Rakh Lai

Guru Amar Daas Ji
Raag Bilaaval
853

ਜਗਤੁ ਜਲੰਦਾ ਰਖਿ ਲੈ ਆਪਣੀ ਕਿਰਪਾ ਧਾਰਿ॥
Jagat jalandaa rakh lai, aapnee kirpaa dhaar

ਜਿਤੁ ਦੁਆਰੈ ਉਬਰੈ ਤਿਤੈ ਲੈਹੁ ਉਬਾਰਿ॥
Jit duaarai ubarai, titai laihu ubaar

ਸਤਿਗੁਰਿ ਸੁਖੁ ਵੇਖਾਲਿਆ ਸਚਾ ਸਬਦੁ ਬੀਚਾਰਿ॥
Satgur sukh vaykhaali-aa, sachaa shabad beechaar

ਨਾਨਕ ਅਵਰੁ ਨ ਸੁਝਈ ਹਰਿ ਬਿਨੁ ਬਖਸਣਹਾਰੁ॥
Naanak avar na soojha-ee, har bin bakhsanhaar

The world is in flames; please bestow Thy mercy.

Save and deliver it, any way You can.

The True Guru has shown the way to peace,
contemplating the True Word.

Nanak knows no other than Thee, O forgiving Lord.

From the *Siri Guru Granth Sahib*, Guru Amar Das ji

Clears Karma: Creates healing energy and
liberation from the bondage of past karma.

Karam Khand Kee Baanee Jor

Guru Nanak Dev Ji
Japji Sahib
Siri Guru Granth Sahib Page 8

ਕਰਮ ਖੰਡ ਕੀ ਬਾਣੀ ਜੋਰੁ॥
Karam khand kee baanee jor

ਤਿਥੈ ਹੋਰੁ ਨ ਕੋਈ ਹੋਰੁ
Tithai hor na ko-ee hor

ਤਿਥੈ ਜੋਧ ਮਹਾਬਲ ਸੂਰ॥
Tithai jodh mahaabal soor

ਤਿਨ ਮਹਿ ਰਾਮੁ ਰਹਿਆ ਭਰਪੂਰ॥
Tin meh raam rahiaa bharpoor

ਤਿਥੈ ਸੀਤੋ ਸੀਤਾ ਮਹਿਮਾ ਮਾਹਿ॥
Tithai seeto seetaa mehmaa maa-eh

ਤਾ ਕੇ ਰੂਪ ਨ ਕਥਨੇ ਜਾਹਿ॥
Taa kay roop na kathanay jaa-eh

ਨਾ ਓਹਿ ਮਰਹਿ ਨ ਠਾਗੇ ਜਾਹਿ॥
Naa oh mareh na thaagay jaa-eh

ਜਿਨ ਕੈ ਰਾਮੁ ਵਸੈ ਮਨ ਮਾਹਿ॥

Jin kai raam vasai man maa-eh

ਤਿਥੈ ਭਗਤ ਵਸਹਿ ਕੇ ਲੋਅ॥

Tithai bhagat vaseh kay loa

ਕਰਹਿ ਅਨੰਦੁ ਸਚਾ ਮਨਿ ਸੋਇ॥

Kareh anand sachaa man so-ei

ਸਚ ਖੰਡਿ ਵਸੈ ਨਿਰੰਕਾਰੁ॥

Sachkhand vasai nirankaar

ਕਰਿ ਕਰਿ ਵੇਖੈ ਨਦਰਿ ਨਿਹਾਲ॥

Kar kar vaykhai nadar nihaal

ਤਿਥੈ ਖੰਡ ਮੰਡਲ ਵਰਭੰਡ॥

Tithai khand mandal varbhand

ਜੇ ਕੋ ਕਥੈ ਤ ਅੰਤ ਨ ਅੰਤ॥

Jay ko kathai ta ant na ant

ਤਿਥੈ ਲੋਅ ਲੋਅ ਆਕਾਰ॥

Tithai loa loa aakaar

ਜਿਵ ਜਿਵ ਹੁਕਮੁ ਤਿਵੈ ਤਿਵ ਕਾਰ ॥
Jiv jiv hukam tivai tiv kaar

ਵੇਖੈ ਵਿਗਸੈ ਕਰਿ ਵੀਚਾਰੁ ॥
Vaykhai vigsai kar veechaar

ਨਾਨਕ ਕਥਨਾ ਕਰੜਾ ਸਾਰੁ ॥
Naanak kathanaa kararaa saar

In the realm of Karma,
the Word is power.

No one else dwells there,
except the warriors of great power,
the spiritual heroes.

They are totally fulfilled,
imbued with the Lord's essence.

Myriads of Sitas are there,
cool and calm in their majestic glory.

Their beauty cannot be described.

Neither death, nor deception,
comes to those in whose heart the Lord abides.

There, the devotees of many worlds abide.

They are full of joy;
their minds are imbued with the True Lord.

In the realm of Truth,
the Formless Lord dwells.

Having created the creation,
He watches over it.

By His glance of Grace,
He bestows happiness.

There are planets,
solar systems, and galaxies.

If one speaks of them,
there is no limit, no end.

There are worlds upon worlds of His creation.

As He commands so do they exist.

He watches over it all,
and contemplating the creation, He rejoices!

O Nanak, to describe this is as hard as steel!

From the *Siri Guru Granth Sahib*, the 37th pauree of
Japji Sahib, Guru Nanak Dev Ji

Clears Karma: Cuts the karma and kills the impact
of all past karma.

Kirpaa Karaho Deen Kay Daatay

Guru Arjan Dev Ji
Raag Raamkalee
882

ਕਿਰਪਾ ਕਰਹੁ ਦੀਨ ਕੇ ਦਾਤੇ ਮੇਰਾ ਗੁਣੁ ਅਵਗਣੁ ਨ ਬੀਚਾਰਹੁ ਕੋਈ॥
Kirpaa karaho deen kay daatay
Mayraa gun avgan na beechaaraho koee.

ਮਾਟੀ ਕਾ ਕਿਆ ਧੋਪੈ ਸੁਆਮੀ ਮਾਨਸ ਕੀ ਗਤਿ ਏਹੀ॥
Maatee kaa kiaa dopai suaamee maanas kee gat ayhee

Having mercy on me,
O Generous Giver, Lord of the meek,
in my supplication You do not consider
my merits and demerits.

Clears Karma: Clears karma and guilt for past deeds.

Saachaa Saahib Sad Miharvaan

Guru Arjan Dev Ji
Raag Sorath
619

ਸਾਚਾ ਸਾਹਿਬੁ ਸਦ ਮਿਹਰਵਾਣ ॥

Saachaa saahib sad miharvaan

The True Lord and Master is
forever merciful and forgiving.

Clears Karma: Absolves you of guilt from past deeds.

Liberation

Ant Na Sifatee

Guru Nanak Dev Ji
Japji Sahib
5

ਅੰਤੁ ਨ ਸਿਫਤੀ ਕਹਣਿ ਨ ਅੰਤੁ॥
Ant na sifatee kehn na ant

ਅੰਤੁ ਨ ਕਰਣੈ ਦੇਣਿ ਨ ਅੰਤੁ॥
Ant na karnai dayn na ant

ਅੰਤੁ ਨ ਵੇਖਣਿ ਸੁਣਣਿ ਨ ਅੰਤੁ॥
Ant na vaykhan sunan na ant

ਅੰਤੁ ਨ ਜਾਪੈ ਕਿਆ ਮਨਿ ਮੰਤੁ॥
Ant na jaapai kiaa man mant

ਅੰਤੁ ਨ ਜਾਪੈ ਕੀਤਾ ਆਕਾਰੁ॥
Ant na jaapai keetaa aakaar

ਅੰਤੁ ਨ ਜਾਪੈ ਪਾਰਾਵਾਰੁ॥
Ant na jaapai paaraavaar

ਅੰਤ ਕਾਰਣਿ ਕੇਤੇ ਬਿਲਲਾਹਿ॥
Ant kaaran kaytay bilalaa-eh

ਤਾ ਕੇ ਅੰਤ ਨ ਪਾਏ ਜਾਹਿ॥
Taa kay ant na paa-ay jaa-eh

ਏਹੁ ਅੰਤੁ ਨ ਜਾਣੈ ਕੋਇ॥
Ayho ant na jaanai ko-ei

ਬਹੁਤਾ ਕਹੀਐ ਬਹੁਤਾ ਹੋਇ॥
Bahutaa keheeai bahutaa ho-ei

ਵਡਾ ਸਾਹਿਬੁ ਊਚਾ ਥਾਉ॥
Vadaa saahib oochaa thaa-o

ਊਚੇ ਉਪਰਿ ਊਚਾ ਨਾਉ॥
Oochay upar oochaa naa-o

ਏਵਡੁ ਊਚਾ ਹੋਵੈ ਕੋਇ॥
Ayvad oochaa hovai ko-ei

ਤਿਸੁ ਊਚੇ ਕਉ ਜਾਣੈ ਸੋਇ॥
Tis oochay kao jaanai so-ei

ਜੇਵਡੁ ਆਪਿ ਜਾਣੈ ਆਪਿ ਆਪਿ॥
Jayvad aap jaanai aap aap

ਨਾਨਕ ਨਦਰੀ ਕਰਮੀ ਦਾਤਿ॥
Naanak nadaree karamee daat

Limitless His praises, limitless those who speak them.

Limitless are His workings and His givings.

Endless are the sounds and sights.

Limitless are the mysteries of His mind.

Endless is the creation's expanse, here and beyond.

Countless struggle to find His limit;
it cannot be found.

Nobody knows the end; the more that is said,
the more there is to say.

Great is the Lord, high is His abode.

His Name is the highest of the high.

One must gain those heights to know,

He himself knows how vast He is, O Nanak.

It is His gracious glance that can raise a person so high.

From the *Siri Guru Granth Sahib*, the 24th pauree of Japji Sahib,
Guru Nanak Dev Ji

Liberation: Breaks through all limitations with the
force of a thunderbolt.

This mantra is so powerful that it affects
generations. It has the power to kill misfortune.

Har Har Mukanday

ਹਰਿ ਹਰਿ ਮੁਕੰਦੇ ॥
Har Har Mukanday

The Infinite Creator liberates me.

Liberation: Turns challenges into opportunities and removes fear.

This mantra liberates one from mental and emotional blocks.

Jinee Naam Dhiaa-ei-aa

Guru Nanak Dev Ji
Japji Sahib
8

ਜਿਨੀ ਨਾਮੁ ਧਿਆਇਆ ਗਏ ਮਸਕਤਿ ਘਾਲਿ॥
Jinee naam dhiaa-ei-aa gay masakat ghaal

ਨਾਨਕ ਤੇ ਮੁਖ ਉਜਲੇ ਕੇਤੀ ਛੁਟੀ ਨਾਲਿ॥
Naanak tay mukh ujalay kaytee chutee naal

Those who recited Naam, they put in the hard labor.

Nanak, their own faces glow, they earn respect, and
they are honored in the Court of the Lord.
Along with themselves, they liberate many others.

Liberation: To direct your mind to a higher frequency.

Jis Daa Saahib Daadhaa Ho-ei

Guru Amar Daas Ji
Raag Bilaaval
842

ਜਿਸ ਦਾ ਸਾਹਿਬੁ ਡਾਢਾ ਹੋਇ ॥
Jis daa saahib daadhaa ho-ei

ਤਿਸ ਨੋ ਮਾਰਿ ਨ ਸਾਕੈ ਕੋਇ ॥
Tis no maar na saakai ko-ei

One who belongs to the All-Powerful Lord and
Master no one can destroy.

Liberation: To bring inner strength and release
from worldly attachments.

Simar Simar Prabh Aapnaa

Guru Arjan Dev Ji
Raag Bilaaval
818

ਸਿਮਰਿ ਸਿਮਰਿ ਪ੍ਰਭੁ ਆਪਨਾ ਨਾਥਾ ਦੁਖ ਥਾਉ ॥
Simar simar prabh aapnaa naathaa dukh thaa-o.

Remembering, remembering my God in meditation,
the house of pain is removed.

Liberation: Removes mental blocks and takes
away suffering.

Teerath Naavaa Jay Tis Bhaavaa

Guru Nanak Dev Ji
Japji Sahib
2

ਤੀਰਥਿ ਨਾਵਾ ਜੇ ਤਿਸੁ ਭਾਵਾ
Teerath naavaa jay tis bhaavaa

ਵਿਣੁ ਭਾਣੇ ਕਿ ਨਾਇ ਕਰੀ ॥
Vin bhaanay kee naa-ei karee

ਜੇਤੀ ਸਿਰਠਿ ਉਪਾਈ ਵੇਖਾ
Jaytee sirath upaa-ee vaykhaa

ਵਿਣੁ ਕਰਮਾ ਕਿ ਮਿਲੈ ਲਈ ॥
Vin karmaa ki milai la-ee

ਮਤਿ ਵਿਚਿ ਰਤਨ ਜਵਾਹਰ ਮਾਣਿਕ
Mat vich ratan javaahar maanik

ਜੇ ਇਕ ਗੁਰ ਕੀ ਸਿਖ ਸੁਣੀ ॥
Jay eik gur kee sikh sunee

ਗੁਰਾ ਇਕ ਦੇਹਿ ਬੁਝਾਈ ॥
Guraa eik dayh bujhaa-ee

ਸਭਨਾ ਜੀਆ ਕਾ ਇਕੁ ਦਾਤਾ

Sabhanaa jee-aa kaa eik daataa

ਸੋ ਮੈ ਵਿਸਰਿ ਨ ਜਾਈ॥

So mai visar na jaa-ee

If I am pleasing to Him,
then that is my pilgrimage and cleansing bath.

Without pleasing Him,
what good are ritual cleansings?

Gazing upon the created beings,
without the karma of good actions,

what are they given to receive?

Within the mind are gems, jewels, and rubies,

from listening to the Guru's teachings, even once.

The Guru has taught me one thing:

There is only the One, the Giver of all souls.

May I never forget Him!

From the *Siri Guru Granth Sahib*, the 6th pauree of Japji Sahib,
Guru Nanak Dev Ji.

Liberation: Dispels limitations.

Recite this pauree when you feel limited,
cornered, trapped, or coerced.

Love

Mangal Saaj Bhaei-aa
Prabh Apnaa Gaaei-aa Raam

Guru Arjan Dev Ji
Raag Bilaaval
845

ਮੰਗਲ ਸਾਜੁ ਭਇਆ ਪ੍ਰਭੁ ਅਪਨਾ ਗਾਇਆ ਰਾਮ ॥

Mangal saaj bhaei-aa prabh apnaa gaaei-aa raam

ਅਬਿਨਾਸੀ ਵਰੁ ਸੁਣਿਆ ਮਨਿ ਉਪਜਿਆ ਚਾਇਆ ਰਾਮ ॥

Abinaasee var suniaa man upajiaa chaaei-aa raam

ਮਨਿ ਪ੍ਰੀਤਿ ਲਾਗੈ ਵਡੈ ਭਾਗੈ ਕਬ ਮਿਲੀਐ ਪੂਰਨ ਪਤੇ ॥

Man preet laagai vadai bhaagai kab milee-ai pooran patay

ਸਹਜੇ ਸਮਾਈਐ ਗੋਵਿੰਦੁ ਪਾਈਐ ਦੇਹੁ ਸਖੀਏ ਮੋਹਿ ਮਤੇ ॥

Sehjay samaaee-ai govind paaee-ai dayho sakhee-ay moeh matay

ਦਿਨੁ ਰੈਨਿ ਠਾਢੀ ਕਰਉ ਸੇਵਾ ਪ੍ਰਭੁ ਕਵਨ ਜੁਗਤੀ ਪਾਇਆ ॥

Din rain thaadhee karao sayvaa prabh kavan jugatee paaei-aa

ਬਿਨਵੰਤਿ ਨਾਨਕ ਕਰਹੁ ਕਿਰਪਾ ਲੈਹੁ ਮੋਹਿ ਲੜਿ ਲਾਇਆ ॥

Binvant naanak karaho kirpaa laiho moeh lar laaei-aa

The time of rejoicing has come; I sing of my Lord God.

I have heard of my Imperishable Husband Lord,
and happiness fills my mind.

My mind is in love with Him;
when shall I realize my great good fortune,

And meet with my Perfect Husband?

If only I could meet the Lord of the Universe,

and be automatically absorbed into Him.

Tell me how, O my companions!

Day and night, I stand and serve my Lord;
how can I attain Him?

Prays Nanak, have mercy on me,
and attach me to the hem of Your robe, O Lord.

From the *Siri Guru Granth Sahib*, Guru Arjan Dev Ji.

Love: To help you find your soulmate and
overcome loneliness.

Sat Kartaar

ਸਤਿ ਕਰਤਾਰ ॥
Sat Kartaar

God is the Doer

Heart Chakra: To open the heart center.

Sat Kartaar is the mantra that Guru Nanak would speak when things would happen, good or bad. His response was, Sat Kartaar! In effect he was saying: "The Great Divine One is the One doing this action in this situation."

Sat (meaning essence of truth, or being) first identifies in the mantra the soul's True Sound. *Kartaar* (meaning 'doer') combines with *Sat* to form a phrase meaning 'One Doer', 'True Manifester' or 'Deliverer of the Truth'. When these primal sounds are repeated over time, we are in effect opening, expanding, and directing the energetic flow of the pranic center of the heart.

The second aspect of this heart-opening mantra
is that it is a key to living in a state of faith. We are
calling on our conscious mind to dwell in harmony
with our soul-mind in the understanding that the
Divine Doer is working in all situations. When we
open ourselves to that flow, then we establish and
allow a path for the Universe to flow through our
lives. By merging our individual will with Divine
Will, we experience the trust and flow of the
Divine, creating infinite miracles in our lives.

Mastery

Ardaas Sunee Daataar

Guru Arjan Dev Ji
Raag Bilaaval
818

ਅਰਦਾਸਿ ਸੁਣੀ ਦਾਤਾਰਿ ਪ੍ਰਭਿ ਹੋਏ ਕਿਰਪਾਲ॥
Ardaas sunee daataar prabh ho-ay kirpaal.

God, the Great Giver, has become merciful;
God has listened to my prayer.

Mastery: To bring mastery of self.

Miracles

Dhann Dhann Raam Daas Gur

Bhatt Sathaa & Balvand
Raag Raamkalee
968

ਧੰਨੁ ਧੰਨੁ ਰਾਮਦਾਸ ਗੁਰ ਜਿਨਿ ਸਿਰਿਆ ਤਿਨੈ ਸਵਾਰਿਆ ॥
Dhann dhann Raam Daas Gur jin siriaa tinai savaariaa

ਪੂਰੀ ਹੋਈ ਕਰਾਮਾਤਿ ਆਪਿ ਸਿਰਜਣਹਾਰੈ ਧਾਰਿਆ ॥
Pooree hoee karaamaat aap sirjanhaarai dhaariaa.

ਸਿਖੀ ਅਤੈ ਸੰਗਤੀ ਪਾਰਬ੍ਰਹਮੁ ਕਰਿ ਨਮਸਕਾਰਿਆ ॥
Sikhee atai sangatee paarbrahm kar namasakaariaa

ਅਟਲੁ ਅਥਾਹੁ ਅਤੋਲੁ ਤੂ ਤੇਰਾ ਅੰਤੁ ਨ ਪਾਰਾਵਾਰਿਆ ॥
Atal athaaho atol too tayraa ant na paaraavaariaa.

ਜਿਨੀ ਤੂੰ ਸੇਵਿਆ ਭਾਉ ਕਰਿ ਸੇ ਤੁਧੁ ਪਾਰਿ ਉਤਾਰਿਆ ॥
Jinee too(n) sayviaa bhaao kar say tudh paar utaariaa

ਲਬੁ ਲੋਭੁ ਕਾਮੁ ਕ੍ਰੋਧੁ ਮੋਹੁ ਮਾਰਿ ਕਢੇ ਤੁਧੁ ਸਪਰਵਾਰਿਆ ॥
Lab lobh kaam krodh moho maar kadhay tudh saparvaariaa

ਧੰਨੁ ਸੁ ਤੇਰਾ ਥਾਨੁ ਹੈ ਸਚੁ ਤੇਰਾ ਪੈਸਕਾਰਿਆ ॥
Dhann so tayraa thaan hai sach tayraa paiskaariaa

ਨਾਨਕੁ ਤੂ ਲਹਣਾ ਤੂਹੈ ਗੁਰੁ ਅਮਰੁ ਤੂ ਵੀਚਾਰਿਆ ॥

Naanak too Lahnaa too hai Gur Amar too veechaariaa.

ਗੁਰੁ ਡਿਠਾ ਤਾਂ ਮਨੁ ਸਾਧਾਰਿਆ ॥ 7 ॥

Gur dithaa taa man saadhaariaa

Blessed, blessed is Guru Ram Das;
the One who created You, has also exalted You.

Perfect is Your miracle;
the Creator Lord Himself has installed You on the throne.

The Sikhs and all the congregation recognize You as
Supreme Lord God, and bow to You.

You are unchanging, unfathomable, and immeasurable;
You have no end or limitation.

Those who serve You with love are carried across.

Greed, envy, sexual desire, anger, and emotional attachment –
You have beaten them and driven them out.

Blessed is Your place,
and true is Your magnificent glory.

You are Nanak, You are Angad,
and You are Amar Das; so do l recognize You.

When l saw the Guru,
then my mind was comforted and consoled.

Miracles: Creates miracles of transformation for any situation of life.

Chanting this mantra makes the impossible become possible, including problems in love, relationships, prosperity, health, healing, or any challenges or difficulties. In times of tragedy, there is one mantra, the miracle mantra, which lives in the realm of the heart and operates on a frequency beyond comprehension. This mantra brings in the miraculous frequency of Guru Ram Das, who is known as the Lord of Miracles.

Peace

Abhang Hai(n) Anang Hai(n)

Guru Gobind Singh
Dasam Granth
Jaap Sahib

ਅਭੰਗ ਹੈਂ ॥ ਅਨੰਗ ਹੈਂ ॥ ਅਭੇਖ ਹੈਂ ॥ ਅਲੇਖ ਹੈਂ ॥
Abhang hai(n). Anang hai(n). Abhaykh hai(n). Alaykh hai(n).

ਅਭਰਮ ਹੈਂ ॥ ਅਕਰਮ ਹੈਂ ॥ ਅਨਾਦਿ ਹੈਂ ॥ ਜੁਗਾਦਿ ਹੈਂ ॥
Abharm hai(n). Akarm hai(n). Anaad hai(n). Jugaad hai(n).

ਅਜੈ ਹੈਂ ॥ ਅਬੈ ਹੈਂ ॥ ਅਭੂਤ ਹੈਂ ॥ ਅਧੂਤ ਹੈਂ ॥
Ajai hai(n). Abai hai(n). Abhoot hai(n). Adhoot hai(n).

ਅਨਾਸ ਹੈਂ ॥ ਉਦਾਸ ਹੈਂ ॥ ਅਧੰਧ ਹੈਂ ॥ ਅਬੰਧ ਹੈਂ ॥
Anaas hai(n). Udaas hai(n). Adhandh hai(n). Abandh hai(n).

ਅਭਗਤ ਹੈਂ ॥ ਬਿਰਕਤ ਹੈਂ ॥ ਅਨਾਸ ਹੈਂ ॥ ਪ੍ਰਕਾਸ ਹੈਂ ॥
Abhagat hai(n). Birakat hai(n). Anaas hai(n). Prakaas hai(n).

ਨਿਚਿੰਤ ਹੈਂ ॥ ਸੁਨਿੰਤ ਹੈਂ ॥ ਅਲਿੱਖ ਹੈਂ ॥ ਅਦਿੱਖ ਹੈਂ ॥
Nichint hai(n). Sunint hai(n). Alikh hai(n). Adikh hai(n).

ਅਲੇਖ ਹੈਂ ॥ ਅਭੇਖ ਹੈਂ ॥ ਅਢਾਹ ਹੈਂ ॥ ਅਗਾਹ ਹੈਂ ॥
Alaykh hai(n). Abhaykh hai(n). Adhaah hai(n). Agaah hai(n).

ਅਸੰਭ ਹੈਂ॥ ਅਗੰਭ ਹੈਂ॥ ਅਨੀਲ ਹੈਂ॥ ਅਨਾਦਿ ਹੈਂ॥
Asanbh hai(n). Aganbh hai(n). Aneel hai(n). Anaad hai(n).

ਅਨਿੱਤ ਹੈਂ॥ ਸੁਨਿੱਤ ਹੈਂ॥ ਅਜਾਤਿ ਹੈਂ॥ ਅਜਾਦਿ ਹੈਂ॥
Anit hai(n). Sunit hai(n). Ajaat hai(n). Ajaad hai(n).

Imperishable, incorporeal, unattired, and indescribable

Indubitable and beyond customary observances
Existing even before the beginning

Impregnable, indestructible, non-substantial, and unshaken

Imperishable, beyond love and affection
Free from worldly entanglements and ties

Impartial to all, free from all attachments
Imperishable, the light of lights

Without anxiety, perpetual existence
Beyond portraiture, invisible

Indescribable, unattired, impregnable, unfathomable

Imperceptible, beyond approach
Beyond colour, form and beginning

Exceptional and unique, ever existing
Unborn and independent

Peace: Opens the heart to mutual understanding and a path to peace.

Chanting this mantra breaks down walls of misunderstanding, deception, and non-cooperation.

Aagai Sukh Mayray Meetaa

Guru Arjan Dev Ji
Raag Sorath
629

ਆਗੈ ਸੁਖੁ ਮੇਰੇ ਮੀਤਾ
Aagai sukh mayray meetaa

ਪਾਛੇ ਆਨਦੁ ਪ੍ਰਭਿ ਕੀਤਾ॥
Paachay aanad prabh keetaa

ਪਰਮੇਸੁਰਿ ਬਣਤ ਬਣਾਈ॥
Parmaysur banat banaa-ee

ਫਿਰਿ ਡੋਲਤ ਕਤਹੂ ਨਾਹੀ॥
Fir dolat katahoo naahee

Peace in this world, O my friends;

bliss in the world hereafter.

The Creator Lord has given me this

and made these arrangements.

Peace: A supplication for peace on earth,
happiness and good will to all people.

Aval Alah

Bhagat Kabeer Ji
Raag Prabhaatee
1349

ਅਵਲਿ ਅਲਹ ਨੂਰੁ ਉਪਾਇਆ ਕੁਦਰਤਿ ਕੇ ਸਭ ਬੰਦੇ॥
Aval alah noor upaaei-aa kudrat kay sabh banday

ਏਕ ਨੂਰ ਤੇ ਸਭੁ ਜਗੁ ਉਪਜਿਆ ਕਉਨ ਭਲੇ ਕੋ ਮੰਦੇ॥
Ayk noor tay sabh jag upajiaa kaon bhalay ko manday

ਲੋਗਾ ਭਰਮਿ ਨ ਭੂਲਹੁ ਭਾਈ॥
Logaa bharam na bhoolaho bhaa-ee

ਖਾਲਿਕੁ ਖਲਕ ਖਲਕ ਖਲਕ ਮਹਿ ਖਾਲਿਕੁ ਪੂਰਿ ਰਹਿਓ ਸ੍ਰਬ ਠਾਂਈ॥ ਰਹਾਉ॥
Khaalik khalak khalak khalak meh khaalik poor raeh-o sarab thaa-ee ‖ Rahaao

ਮਾਟੀ ਏਕ ਅਨੇਕ ਭਾਂਤਿ ਕਰਿ ਸਾਜੀ ਸਾਜਨਹਾਰੈ॥
Maatee ayk anayk bhaant kar saajee saajanahaarai.

ਨਾ ਕਛੁ ਪੋਚ ਮਾਟੀ ਕੇ ਭਾਂਡੇ ਨਾ ਕਛੁ ਪੋਚ ਕੁੰਭਾਰੈ॥
Naa kachh poch maatee kay bhaanday naa kachh poch kumbhaarai

ਸਭ ਮਹਿ ਸਚਾ ਏਕੋ ਸੋਈ ਤਿਸ ਕਾ ਕੀਆ ਸਭੁ ਕਛੁ ਹੋਈ ॥
Sabh meh sachaa ayko soee tis kaa kee-aa sabh kachh hoee

ਹੁਕਮੁ ਪਛਾਨੈ ਸੁ ਏਕੋ ਜਾਨੈ ਬੰਦਾ ਕਹੀਐ ਸੋਈ ॥
Hukam pachhaanai so ayko jaanai bandaa kahee-ai soee

ਅਲਹੁ ਅਲਖੁ ਨ ਜਾਈ ਲਖਿਆ ਗੁਰਿ ਗੁੜੁ ਦੀਨਾ ਮੀਠਾ ॥
Alaho alakh na jaa-ee lakhiaa gur gur deenaa meethaa

ਕਹਿ ਕਬੀਰ ਮੇਰੀ ਸੰਕਾ ਨਾਸੀ ਸਰਬ ਨਿਰੰਜਨੁ ਡੀਠਾ ॥
Keh Kabeer mayree sankaa naasee sarab niranjan deethaa

First Allah created the Light; then by His Creative Power
He made all mortal beings.

From the One Light, the entire universe welled up.
So who is good, and who is bad?

O people, O Siblings of Destiny,
do not wander deluded by doubt.

The Creator and the creation are one,
totally pervading and permeating all places. Pause

The clay is the same,
but the Fashioner has fashioned it in various ways.

There is nothing wrong with the pot of clay;
there is nothing wrong with the Potter.

The One True Lord abides in all,
and by His making, everything is made.

Whoever realizes His command, knows the One Lord,
and that person becomes His slave.

The Lord Allah is unseen; He cannot be seen.
The Guru has blessed me with this sweetness.

Says Kabir, my anxiety and fear are gone;
the Immaculate Lord pervades everywhere.

Peace: Brings the consciousness of equality and good will to all.

This is a universal and humanitarian mantra. It was written by the Sufi Saint Kabir, and included in the holy book of the Sikhs, the *Siri Guru Granth Sahib*.

Ayh Vairee Mitar

Guru Arjan Dev Ji
Raag Maaroo
1096

ਏਹ ਵੈਰੀ ਮਿਤੁ ਸਭਿ ਕੀਤਿਆ ਨਹ ਮੰਗਹਿ ਮੰਦਾ॥
Ayh vairee mitar sabh keetiaa nah mangeh mandaa

All my enemies have become friends,
and no one wishes me ill.

Peace: Dissolves animosity.

Kar Kirpaa Antarjaamee

Guru Arjan Dev Ji
Raag Sorath
623

ਕਰਿ ਕਿਰਪਾ ਅੰਤਰਜਾਮੀ
Kar kirpaa antarjaamee

ਦਾਸ ਨਾਨਕ ਸਰਨਿ ਸੁਆਮੀ ॥
Daas Naanak saran suaamee

The Inner Knower, the Searcher of Hearts,
has granted mercy.

Slave Nanak seeks the sanctuary of the Divine Master.

Peace: To know that true peace dwells within.

Naanak Prabh Sarnaa-ay

Guru Arjan Dev Ji
Raag Sorath
630

ਨਾਨਕ ਪ੍ਰਭ ਸਰਣਾਏ॥ ਜਿਨਿ ਸਗਲੇ ਰੋਗ ਮਿਟਾਏ॥
Naanak prabh sarnaa-ay Jin sagalay rog mitaa-ay

Nanak has entered God's Sanctuary and
all disease is eradicated.

Peace: Resolves animosity and brings peace of mind.

Raham Tayree Sukh Paaei-aa

Guru Arjan Dev Ji
Raag Tilang
724

ਰਹਮ ਤੇਰੀ ਸੁਖੁ ਪਾਇਆ ਸਦਾ ਨਾਨਕ ਕੀ ਅਰਦਾਸਿ ॥
Raham tayree sukh paaei-aa sadaa Naanak kee ardaas

By Your Mercy, may I find peace;
this is Nanak's lasting prayer.

Peace: Brings peace of mind.

Soee Dhiaa-ee-ai Jeearay

Guru Arjan Dev Ji
Siree Raag
44

ਸੋਈ ਧਿਆਈਐ ਜੀਅੜੇ ਸਿਰਿ ਸਾਹਾਂ ਪਾਤਿਸਾਹੁ ॥

Soee dhiaaee-ai jeearay sir saahaa paatisaaho

ਤਿਸ ਹੀ ਕੀ ਕਰਿ ਆਸ ਮਨ ਜਿਸ ਕਾ ਸਭਸੁ ਵੇਸਾਹੁ ॥

Tis hee kee kar aas man jis kaa sabhas vaysaaho

ਸਭਿ ਸਿਆਣਪਾ ਛਡਿ ਕੈ ਗੁਰ ਕੀ ਚਰਨੀ ਪਾਹੁ ॥

Sabh siaanpaa chhad kai gur kee charnee paaho

ਮਨ ਮੇਰੇ ਸੁਖ ਸਹਜ ਸੇਤੀ ਜਪਿ ਨਾਉ ॥

Man mayray sukh sahaj saytee jap naao

ਆਠ ਪਹਰ ਪ੍ਰਭੁ ਧਿਆਇ ਤੂੰ ਗੁਣ ਗੋਇੰਦ ਨਿਤ ਗਾਉ ॥ 1 ॥ ਰਹਾਉ ॥

Aath pahar prabh dhiaa-ei too(n) gun goind nit gaao || Rahaao

ਤਿਸ ਕੀ ਸਰਨੀ ਪਰੁ ਮਨਾ ਜਿਸੁ ਜੇਵਡੁ ਅਵਰੁ ਨ ਕੋਇ ॥

Tis kee sarnee par manaa jis jayvad avar na ko-ei

ਜਿਸੁ ਸਿਮਰਤ ਸੁਖੁ ਹੋਇ ਘਣਾ ਦੁਖੁ ਦਰਦੁ ਨ ਮੂਲੇ ਹੋਇ ॥

Jis simrat sukh hoei ghanaa dukh darad na moolay ho-ei

ਸਦਾ ਸਦਾ ਕਰਿ ਚਾਕਰੀ ਪ੍ਰਭੁ ਸਾਹਿਬੁ ਸਚਾ ਸੋਇ ॥

Sadaa sadaa kar chaakaree prabh saahib sachaa so-ei

ਸਾਧਸੰਗਤਿ ਹੋਇ ਨਿਰਮਲਾ ਕਟੀਐ ਜਮ ਕੀ ਫਾਸ ॥

Saadh sangat ho-ei nirmalaa katee-ai jam kee faas

ਸੁਖਦਾਤਾ ਭੈ ਭੰਜਨੋ ਤਿਸੁ ਆਗੈ ਕਰਿ ਅਰਦਾਸਿ ॥

Sukhdaataa bhai bhanjano tis aagai kar ardaas

ਮਿਹਰ ਕਰੇ ਜਿਸੁ ਮਿਹਰਵਾਨੁ ਤਾਂ ਕਾਰਜੁ ਆਵੈ ਰਾਸਿ ॥

Mihar karay jis miharvaan taan kaaraj aavai raas

ਬਹੁਤੋ ਬਹੁਤੁ ਵਖਾਨੀਐ ਊਚੋ ਊਚਾ ਥਾਉ ॥

Bahuto bahut vakhaanee-ai oocho oochaa thaao

ਵਰਨਾ ਚਿਹਨਾ ਬਾਹਰਾ ਕੀਮਤਿ ਕਹਿ ਨ ਸਕਾਉ ॥

Varnaa chihnaa baaharaa keemat keh na sakaao

ਨਾਨਕ ਕਉ ਪ੍ਰਭ ਮਇਆ ਕਰਿ ਸਚੁ ਦੇਵਹੁ ਅਪੁਨਾ ਨਾਉ ॥

Naanak kao prabh maei-aa kar sach dayvho apunaa naao

Meditate on Him, O my soul;
He is the Supreme One over earthly kings and emperors.

Place the hopes of your mind in the One,
in whom all have faith.

Give up all your clever tricks,
and grasp the feet of the Guru.

O my mind, chant the Name with
intuitive peace and poise.

Twenty-four hours a day, meditate on God.

Constantly sing the glories of the Lord of the Universe. Pause

Seek His shelter, O my mind;
there is no other as great as He.

Remembering Him in meditation, a profound peace is obtained.
Pain and suffering will not touch you at all.

Forever and ever, work for God;
He is our True Lord and Master.

In the Saadh Sangat, the Company of the Holy,
one becomes absolutely pure,
and the noose of death shall be cut away.

Offer your prayers to Him,
the giver of peace, the destroyer of fear.

Showing His mercy,
the merciful Master shall resolve your affairs.

The Lord is said to be the Greatest of the Great;
His kingdom is the Highest of the High.

He has no color or mark;
His value cannot be estimated.

God, please show mercy to Nanak,
and bless him with Your True Name.

Peace: Meditating on this shabad calms the storm
of the mind to create inner peace.

Prosperity

Amul Gun Amul Vaapaar

Guru Nanak Dev Ji
Japji Sahib
Page 5

ਅਮੁਲ ਗੁਣ ਅਮੁਲ ਵਾਪਾਰ ॥
Amul gun amul vaapaar

ਅਮੁਲ ਵਾਪਾਰੀਏ ਅਮੁਲ ਭੰਡਾਰ ॥
Amul vaapaaree-ay amul bhandaar

ਅਮੁਲ ਆਵਹਿ ਅਮੁਲ ਲੈ ਜਾਹਿ ॥
Amul aaveh amul lai jaa-eh

ਅਮੁਲ ਭਾਇ ਅਮੁਲਾ ਸਮਾਹਿ ॥
Amul bhaa-ei amulaa samaa-eh

ਅਮੁਲੁ ਧਰਮੁ ਅਮੁਲੁ ਦੀਬਾਣੁ ॥
Amul dharam amul deebaan

ਅਮੁਲੁ ਤੁਲੁ ਅਮੁਲੁ ਪਰਵਾਣੁ ॥
Amul tul amul parvaan

ਅਮੁਲੁ ਬਖਸੀਸ ਅਮੁਲੁ ਨੀਸਾਣੁ ॥
Amul bakhsheesh amul neeshaan

ਅਮੁਲੁ ਕਰਮੁ ਅਮੁਲੁ ਫੁਰਮਾਣੁ ॥

Amul karam amul furmaan

ਅਮੁਲੋ ਅਮੁਲੁ ਆਖਿਆ ਨ ਜਾਇ ॥

Amulo amul aakhiaa na jaa-ei

ਆਖਿ ਆਖਿ ਰਹੇ ਲਿਵ ਲਾਇ ॥

Aakh aakh rehay liv laa-ei

ਆਖਹਿ ਵੇਦ ਪਾਠ ਪੁਰਾਣ ॥

Aakheh vayd paath puraan

ਆਖਹਿ ਪੜੇ ਕਰਹਿ ਵਖਿਆਣ ॥

Aakheh paray kareh vakhiaan

ਆਖਹਿ ਬਰਮੇ ਆਖਹਿ ਇੰਦ ॥

Aakheh barmay aakheh ind

ਆਖਹਿ ਗੋਪੀ ਤੈ ਗੋਵਿੰਦ ॥

Aakheh gopee tai govind

ਆਖਹਿ ਈਸਰ ਆਖਹਿ ਸਿਧ ॥

Aakheh eesar aakheh sidh

ਆਖਹਿ ਕੇਤੇ ਕੀਤੇ ਬੁਧ ॥

Aakheh kaytay keetay budh

ਆਖਹਿ ਦਾਨਵ ਆਖਹਿ ਦੇਵ॥

Aakheh daanav aakheh dayv

ਆਖਹਿ ਸੁਰਿ ਨਰ ਮੁਨਿ ਜਨ ਸੇਵ॥

Aakheh sur nar mun jan sayv

ਕੇਤੇ ਆਖਹਿ ਆਖਣਿ ਪਾਹਿ॥

Kaytay aakheh aakhan paa-eh

ਕੇਤੇ ਕਹਿ ਕਹਿ ਉਠਿ ਉਠਿ ਜਾਹਿ॥

Kaytay keh keh uth uth jaa-eh

ਏਤੇ ਕੀਤੇ ਹੋਰਿ ਕਰੇਹਿ॥

Aytay keetay hor karayeh

ਤਾ ਆਖਿ ਨ ਸਕਹਿ ਕੇਈ ਕੇਇ॥

Taa aakh na sakeh kayee kayei

ਜੇਵਡੁ ਭਾਵੈ ਤੇਵਡੁ ਹੋਇ॥

Jayvad bhaavai tayvad ho-ei

ਨਾਨਕ ਜਾਣੈ ਸਾਚਾ ਸੋਇ॥

Naanak jaanai saachaa so-ei

ਜੇ ਕੋ ਆਖੈ ਬੋਲੁਵਿਗਾੜੁ॥

Jay ko aakhai bol vigaar

ਤਾ ਲਿਖੀਐ ਸਿਰਿ ਗਾਵਾਰਾ ਗਾਵਾਰੁ ॥

Taa likhee-ai sir gaavaaraa gaavaar

Priceless are the virtues;
priceless are the dealings.

Priceless are the dealers;
priceless are the treasures.

Priceless are those who
come to the Divine Master.

Priceless are those who
buy from the Divine.

Priceless is the love;
priceless is absorption into the Divine.

Priceless is the Divine Law of Dharma.

Priceless is the Divine Court of Justice.

Priceless are the scales;
priceless are the weights.

Priceless are the blessings;
priceless is the banner and insignia.

Priceless are the actions;
priceless is the royal command.

Priceless, O priceless beyond expression!

Speak of the Divine One continually,
and vibrate the string of Divine Love.

The Vedas and the Puraanas speak.

The scholars speak and lecture.

Brahma speaks, Indra speaks,
the Gopis and Krishna speak.

The many created Buddhas speak.

The demons speak, the demigods speak.

The spiritual warriors,
the angelic beings, the silent sages,

the humble and serviceful speak.

So many speak and try to describe the One.

So many have spoken again and again,

and have then arisen and departed.

Even if the Creator were to create
as many again as there already are,
they still could not describe the One.

His greatness is known only to Him.

O Nanak, the True Master knows.

If someone presumes to describe the One,

That person shall be known as the most foolish of fools!

Prosperity: Transforms misery, loss, and
misfortune into bounty.

This mantra is from the Siri Guru Granth Sahib,
the 26th pauree of Japji Sahib, by Guru Nanak.

Bahutaa Karam

Guru Nanak Dev Ji
Japji Sahib
Page 5

ਬਹੁਤਾ ਕਰਮੁ ਲਿਖਿਆ ਨਾ ਜਾਇ॥
Bahutaa karam likhiaa naa jaa-ei

ਵਡਾ ਦਾਤਾ ਤਿਲੁ ਨ ਤਮਾਇ॥
Vadaa daataa til na tamaa-ei

ਕੇਤੇ ਮੰਗਹਿ ਜੋਧ ਅਪਾਰ॥
Kaytay mangeh jodh apaar

ਕੇਤਿਆ ਗਣਤ ਨਹੀ ਵਿਚਾਰੁ॥
Kaytiaa ganat nahee veechaar

ਕੇਤੇ ਖਪਿ ਤੁਟਹਿ ਵੇਕਾਰ॥
Kaytay khap tuteh vaykaar

ਕੇਤੇ ਲੈ ਲੈ ਮੁਕਰੁ ਪਾਹਿ॥
Kaytay lai lai mukar paa-eh

ਕੇਤੇ ਮੂਰਖ ਖਾਹੀ ਖਾਹਿ॥
Kaytay moorakh khaahee khaa-eh

ਕੇਤਿਆ ਦੂਖ ਭੂਖ ਸਦ ਮਾਰ॥
Kaytiaa dookh bhookh sad maar

ਏਹਿ ਭਿ ਦਾਤਿ ਤੇਰੀ ਦਾਤਾਰ॥
Ay-eh bhi daat tayree daataar

ਬੰਦਿ ਖਲਾਸੀ ਭਾਣੈ ਹੋਇ॥
Band khalaasee bhaanai ho-ei

ਹੋਰੁ ਆਖਿ ਨ ਸਕੈ ਕੋਇ॥
Hor aakh na sakai ko-ei

ਜੇ ਕੋ ਖਾਇਕੁ ਆਖਣਿ ਪਾਇ॥
Jay ko khaa-eik aakhan paa-ei

ਓਹੁ ਜਾਣੈ ਜੇਤੀਆ ਮੁਹਿ ਖਾਇ॥
Oho jaanai jaytee-aa mueh khaa-ei

ਆਪੇ ਜਾਣੈ ਆਪੇ ਦੇਇ॥
Aapay jaanai aapay day-ei

ਆਖਹਿ ਸਿ ਭਿ ਕੇਈ ਕੇਇ॥
Aakheh si bhi kayee kay-ei

ਜਿਸ ਨੋ ਬਖਸੇ ਸਿਫਤਿ ਸਾਲਾਹ ॥
Jis no bakhshay sifat saalaah

ਨਾਨਕ ਪਾਤਿਸਾਹੀ ਪਾਤਿਸਾਹੁ ॥
Naanak paatishaahee paatishaaho

His blessings are so abundant
there can be no written account of them.

The Great Giver does not hold back anything.

So many great, heroic warriors beg at
the door of the Infinite Lord.

So many contemplate and dwell upon Him,
that they cannot be counted.

So many waste away to death engaged in corruption.

So many take and take again, and then deny receiving.

So many foolish consumers keep on consuming.

So many endure distress,
deprivation, and constant abuse.

Even these are Your gifts, O Great Giver!

Liberation from bondage comes only by Your Will.

No one else has any say in this.

If some fool should presume to say that he does,

He shall learn, and feel the effects of his folly.

He Himself knows, He Himself gives.

Few, very few are those who acknowledge this.

One who is blessed to sing the Praises of the Lord,

O Nanak, is the King of kings.

Prosperity: Removes duality to create prosperity and harmony.

This is a powerful mantra from the Siri Guru Granth Sahib, the 25th pauree of Japji Sahib, by Guru Nanak. Recite it eleven times each day to bring prosperity and wealth.

"The 25th pauree adds up to seven. It is a platform of levitation. It means wherever you are and whatever you are, this pauree will elevate you, levitate you, to the point of achievement, no matter what!"

"Prosperity is a state produced immediately by the mind. When the sun comes out of the clouds, everything is lit. When the mind comes out of duality, prosperity is there. The 25th pauree has the power to take away duality because it covers every aspect of the projection of the self. It works on the tenth body, the radiant body."

– Yogi Bhajan
© The Teachings of Yogi Bhajan, July 23, 1986

Har Har Har Har Gobinday

ਹਰਿ ਹਰਿ ਹਰਿ ਹਰਿ ਗੋਬਿੰਦੇ
Har Har Har Har Gobinday

ਹਰਿ ਹਰਿ ਹਰਿ ਹਰਿ ਮੁਕੰਦੇ
Har Har Har Har Mukanday

ਹਰਿ ਹਰਿ ਹਰਿ ਹਰਿ ਉਧਾਰੇ
Har Har Har Har Udhaaray

ਹਰਿ ਹਰਿ ਹਰਿ ਹਰਿ ਅਪਾਰੇ
Har Har Har Har Apaaray

ਹਰਿ ਹਰਿ ਹਰਿ ਹਰਿ ਹਰੀਅੰ
Har Har Har Har Haree-ang

ਹਰਿ ਹਰਿ ਹਰਿ ਹਰਿ ਕਰੀਅੰ
Har Har Har Har Karee-ang

ਹਰਿ ਹਰਿ ਹਰਿ ਹਰਿ ਨਿਨਾਮੇ
Har Har Har Har Nirnaamay

ਹਰਿ ਹਰਿ ਹਰਿ ਹਰਿ ਅਕਾਮੇ
Har Har Har Har Akaamay

Ever Present Sustainer

Ever Present Liberator

Ever Present Enlightener

Ever Present Immortal

Ever Present Destroyer

Ever Present Creator

Ever Present Nameless One

Ever Present Desireless One

Prosperity: Brings in all that you need.

This mantra attunes the mind to prosperity. Opportunities, money, and richness will come.

Jai Jai Kaar Jag Gaavai

Guru Arjan Dev Ji
Raag Sorath
Page 623

ਜੈ ਜੈ ਕਾਰੁ ਜਗੁ ਗਾਵੈ ॥

Jai jai kaar jag gaavai

ਮਨ ਚਿੰਦਿਅੜੇ ਫਲ ਪਾਵੈ ॥

Man chindiaray fal paavai

The world sings cheers of victory.

The fruits of my hopes and dreams are obtained.

Prosperity: Brings wealth, prosperity and inner fulfillment.

Jap Man Sat Naam

Guru Ram Das Ji
Raag Dhanaasree
Page 670

ਜਪਿ ਮਨ ਸਤਿ ਨਾਮੁ ਸਦਾ ਸਤਿ ਨਾਮ॥
ਸਤਿ ਨਾਮੁ ਸਤਿ ਨਾਮ ਸਤਿ ਨਾਮੁ ਸਦਾ ਸਤਿ ਨਾਮ॥

Jap Man Sat Naam, Sadaa Sat Naam,
Sat Naam, Sat Naam, Sat Naam Sadaa Sat Naam

ਇਛਾ ਪੂਰਕੁ ਸਰਬ ਸੁਖਦਾਤਾ ਹਰਿ ਜਾ ਕੈ ਵਸਿ ਹੈ ਕਾਮਧੇਨਾ॥

Eichh-aa poorak sarab sukhdaataa har jaa kai vas hai kaamdhay-naa

ਸੋ ਐਸਾ ਹਰਿ ਧਿਆਈਐ ਮੇਰੇ ਜੀਅੜੇ ਤਾ ਸਰਬ ਸੁਖ ਪਾਵਹਿ ਮੇਰੇ ਮਨਾ॥

So aisaa har dhiaaee-ai mayray jeearay taa
sarab sukh paaveh mayray manaa

ਜਪਿ ਮਨ ਸਤਿ ਨਾਮੁ ਸਦਾ ਸਤਿ ਨਾਮੁ॥ ਹਲਤਿ ਪਲਤਿ ਮੁਖ ਊਜਲ ਹੋਈ ਹੈ

Jap man sat naam sadaa sat naam. Halat palat mukh oojal hoee hai

ਨਿਤ ਧਿਆਈਐ ਹਰਿ ਪੁਰਖੁ ਨਿਰੰਜਨਾ॥ ਰਹਾਉ॥

Nit dhiaaee-ai har purakh niranjanaa. Rahaao

ਜਹ ਹਰਿ ਸਿਮਰਨੁ ਭਇਆ ਤਹ ਉਪਾਧਿ ਗਤੁ ਕੀਨੀ ਵਡਭਾਗੀ ਹਰਿ ਜਪਨਾ॥

**Jeh har simran bhaei-aa teh upaadh gat keenee
vadabhaagee har japanaa**

ਜਨ ਨਾਨਕ ਕਉ ਗੁਰਿ ਇਹ ਮਤਿ ਦੀਨੀ ਜਪਿ ਹਰਿ ਭਵਜਲੁ ਤਰਨਾ॥

Jan naanak kao gur eih mat deenee jap har bhavajal taranaa

Oh my mind, chant the True Name, Sat Naam, the True Name.

The Lord is the Fulfiller of desires,
the Giver of total peace;
the Kaamdhaynaa, the mythical cow which fulfills all wishes,
is in His power.

So meditate on such a Lord, Oh my soul.
Then, you shall obtain total peace, Oh my mind.

Oh my mind, chant the True Name,
Sat Naam, the True Name.

In this world, and in the world beyond, your face shall be radiant,
by meditating continually on the immaculate Lord God.

Wherever anyone remembers the Lord in meditation,
disaster runs away from that place.
By great good fortune, we meditate on the Lord.

The Guru has blessed servant Nanak with this understanding,
that by meditating on the Lord,
we cross over the terrifying world ocean.

From the *Siri Guru Granth Sahib*, Guru Ram Das.

Prosperity: Opens one to the infinite flow of prosperity.

This shabad brings the joy of merging with the Divine and opens one to the infinite flow of prosperity by attuning the mind to the creative power of Infinity.

Jaa Too Mayrai Val Hai

Guru Arjan Dev Ji
RAag Maaroo
Page 1096

ਜਾ ਤੂ ਮੇਰੈ ਵਲਿ ਹੈ ਤਾ ਕਿਆ ਮੁਹਛੰਦਾ॥
Jaa too mayrai val hai taa kiaa muhachhandaa .

ਤੁਧੁ ਸਭੁ ਕਿਛੁ ਮੈਨੋ ਸਉਪਿਆ ਜਾ ਤੇਰਾ ਬੰਦਾ॥
Tudh sabh kichh maino saupiaa jaa tayraa bandaa.

ਲਖਮੀ ਤੋਟਿ ਨ ਆਵਈ ਖਾਇ ਖਰਚਿ ਰਹੰਦਾ॥
Lakhmee tot na aavaee khaa-ei kharach rahandaa.

ਲਖ ਚਉਰਾਸੀਹ ਮੇਦਨੀ ਸਭ ਸੇਵ ਕਰੰਦਾ॥
Lakh chaoraaseh maydanee sabh sayv karandaa.

When You are on my side, Lord,
what do I need to worry about?

You entrusted everything to me,
when I became Your slave.

My wealth is inexhaustible,
no matter how much I spend and consume.

The 8.4 million species of beings
all work to serve me.

Prosperity: Removes subconscious blocks to
allow prosperity and abundance to flow.

Kar Saant Sukh Man Aa-ei Vasiaa

Guru Amar Das Ji
Raag Ramkalee
Page 917

ਕਰਿ ਸਾਂਤਿ ਸੁਖ ਮਨਿ ਆਇ ਵਸਿਆ ਜਿਨਿ ਇਛਾ ਸਭਿ ਪੁਜਾਈਆ॥
Kar saant sukh man aa-ei vasiaa jin eichhaa sabh pujaa-ee-aa.

Peace and tranquility fill my mind;
all my desires are fulfilled.

Prosperity: All blessings, prosperity, and
abundance flow into your life.

Keetaa Loree-ai Kam

Guru Nanak Dev Ji
Siree Raag
Page 91

ਕੀਤਾ ਲੋੜੀਐ ਕੰਮੁ ਸੁ ਹਰਿ ਪਹਿ ਆਖੀਐ ॥
Keetaa loree-ai kam, so har peh aakhee-ai

ਕਾਰਜੁ ਦੇਇ ਸਵਾਰਿ ਸਤਿਗੁਰ ਸਚੁ ਸਾਖੀਐ ॥
Kaaraj dayei savaar satgur sach saakhee-ai

ਸੰਤਾ ਸੰਗਿ ਨਿਧਾਨੁ ਅੰਮ੍ਰਿਤੁ ਚਾਖੀਐ ॥
Santaa sang nidhaan amrit chaakhee-ai

ਭੈ ਭੰਜਨ ਮਿਹਰਵਾਨ ਦਾਸ ਕੀ ਰਾਖੀਐ ॥
Bhai bhanjan miharvaan daas kee raakhee-ai

ਨਾਨਕ ਹਰਿ ਗੁਣ ਗਾਇ ਅਲਖੁ ਪ੍ਰਭੁ ਲਾਖੀਐ ॥
Naanak har gun gaa-ei alakh prabh laakhee-ai

Tell the Lord the work you wish to accomplish;

by the True Guru's Word,
your affairs shall be resolved.

You shall taste the ambrosial nectar in
the company of Saints.

The merciful Lord is the destroyer of fear,
and protector of His slaves.

O Nanak, sing the praises of the Lord,
and see the unseen Lord.

From the *Siri Guru Granth Sahib*, Guru Nanak Dev Ji

Prosperity: Brings countless blessings, prosperity,
and abundance.

Mitar Piaaray Noo(n)

Guru Gobind Singh Ji
Dasam Granth
Page 1541

ਮਿਤ੍ਰ ਪਿਆਰੇ ਨੂੰ ਹਾਲੁ ਮੁਰੀਦਾਂ ਦਾ ਕਹਣਾ॥
Mitar piaaray noo(n) haal mureedaa daa kahanaa

ਤੁਧੁ ਬਿਨੁ ਰੋਗੁ ਰਜਾਈਆ ਦਾ ਓਢਣ ਨਾਗ ਨਿਵਾਸਾ ਦੇ ਰਹਣਾ॥
Tudh bin rog rajaaee-aa daa odhan
naag nivaasaa day rahanaa

ਸੂਲ ਸੁਰਾਹੀ ਖੰਜਰੁ ਪਿਆਲਾ ਬਿੰਗ ਕਸਾਈਆ ਦਾ ਸਹਣਾ॥
Sool suraahee khanjar piaalaa bing kasaaee-aa daa sahanaa

ਯਾਰੜੇ ਦਾ ਸਾਨੂੰ ਸਥਰੁ ਚੰਗਾ ਭਠ ਖੇੜਿਆ ਦਾ ਰਹਣਾ॥
Yaararray daa saanoo(n) sathar changaa
bhath khayriaa daa rahanaa

Without You, rich blankets are a disease and
the comfort of the house is like living with snakes.

Our water pitchers are like stakes of torture and
our cups have edges like daggers.

Your neglect is like the suffering of
animals at the hands of butchers.

Our Beloved Lord's straw bed is more pleasing to us
than living in costly mansions.

From the Dasam Granth of the Tenth Master,
Guru Gobind Singh Ji

Prosperity: Brings relief from debts and
the fulfillment of wealth and prosperity.

Prithvee Hai Aakaash Hai – Isht Sodhana Mantra

ਪ੍ਰਿਥਵੀ ਹੈ ਆਕਾਸ਼ ਹੈ ਗੁਰੂ ਰਾਮ ਦਾਸ ਹੈ ॥
Prithvee Hai Aakaash Hai Guroo Raam Daas Hai

The Earth is, The Heavens are, Guru Ram Das is.

Prosperity: Makes you present and attracts opportunities for prosperity.

This mantra calls on your highest spirit and keeps you humble and effective in your new ventures. This is another version of the Isht Sodhana Mantra, recited as *"Dhartee Hai, Aakaash Hai, Guroo Raam Daas Hai."* Practice this mantra with visualization to connect the earth and the vastness of the ethers. Project the mantra from the heart.

Saachaa Saahib Saach Naa-ei

Guru Nanak Dev Ji
Japji Sahib
Page 2

ਸਾਚਾ ਸਾਹਿਬੁ ਸਾਚੁ ਨਾਇ ਭਾਖਿਆ ਭਾਉ ਅਪਾਰੁ ॥
Saachaa saahib saach naa-ei bhaakhiaa bhaao apaar

ਆਖਹਿ ਮੰਗਹਿ ਦੇਹਿ ਦੇਹਿ ਦਾਤਿ ਕਰੇ ਦਾਤਾਰੁ ॥
Aakheh mangeh dayeh dayeh daat karay daataar

ਫੇਰਿ ਕਿ ਅਗੈ ਰਖੀਐ ਜਿਤੁ ਦਿਸੈ ਦਰਬਾਰੁ ॥
Fayr ki agai rakhee-ai jit disai darbaar

ਮੁਹੌ ਕਿ ਬੋਲਣੁ ਬੋਲੀਐ ਜਿਤੁ ਸੁਣਿ ਧਰੇ ਪਿਆਰੁ ॥
Muhaao ki bolan bolee-ai jit sun dharay piaar

ਅੰਮ੍ਰਿਤ ਵੇਲਾ ਸਚੁ ਨਾਉ ਵਡਿਆਈ ਵੀਚਾਰੁ ॥
Amrit vaylaa sach naao vadiaa-ee veechaar

ਕਰਮੀ ਆਵੈ ਕਪੜਾ ਨਦਰੀ ਮੋਖੁ ਦੁਆਰੁ ॥
Karmee aavai kapraa nadaree mokh duaar

ਨਾਨਕ ਏਵੈ ਜਾਣੀਐ ਸਭੁ ਆਪੇ ਸਚਿਆਰੁ ॥
Naanak ayvai jaanee-ai sabh aapay sachiaar

True is the Master, true is His name,
spoken with Infinite love.

People beg and pray, "Give to us, give to us,"
and the Great Giver keeps giving His gifts.

What then, should we place in offering before Him,
by which we might see His court?

And which words should we utter, that by hearing them,
His love might be evoked?

In the Amrit Vela,
the ambrosial hours before the dawn,

chant the True Name,
and reflect deeply upon His glorious greatness.

By the karma of your past actions,
the robe of this physical body has been obtained.

By His grace, the gate of liberation is found.

O Nanak, know this well. The True One,
Himself, is All in all.

From the *Siri Guru Granth Sahib*, the 4th pauree of Japji Sahib,
Guru Nanak Dev Ji

Prosperity: Blesses those trapped in feelings of
poverty and lack of means.

Sat Naam Sat Naam Sat Naam
Sat Naam Sat Naam Sat Naam
Whaa-hay Guroo

ਸਤਿ ਨਾਮ ਸਤਿ ਨਾਮ ਸਤਿ ਨਾਮ ਸਤਿ ਨਾਮ ਸਤਿ ਨਾਮ ਸਤਿ ਨਾਮ ਵਾਹਿ ਗੁਰੂ
Sat Naam Sat Naam Sat Naam Sat Naam
Sat Naam Sat Naam Whaa-hay Guroo

Truth is my identity.
Indescrible ecstasy flows from Guru's wisdom.

Prosperity: Brings prosperity and balance.

This mantra is rhythmic and entrancing. It helps balance the nervous system, eliminating blocks to receiving your prosperity.

Protection

Ab Rachhaa Mayree Tum Karo

Guru Gobind Singh Ji
Dasam Granth
Page 1722

ਅਬ ਰੱਛਾ ਮੇਰੀ ਤੁਮ ਕਰੋ॥
Ab rachhaa mayree tum karo

ਸਿੱਖ ਉਬਾਰਿ ਅਸਿੱਖ ਸੰਘਰੋ॥
Sikh ubaar asikh sangharo

Please, protect me now.

Those who follow You are saved,
and those who do not are lost.

Protection: For protection in all aspects of life.

Aad Guray Nameh

Guru Arjan Dev Ji
Raag Gauree
Page 262

ਆਦਿ ਗੁਰਏ ਨਮਹ ॥
Aad Guray Nameh

ਜੁਗਾਦਿ ਗੁਰਏ ਨਮਹ ॥
Jugaad Guray Nameh

ਸਤਿਗੁਰਏ ਨਮਹ ॥
Sat Guray Nameh

ਸ੍ਰੀ ਗੁਰਦੇਵਏ ਨਮਹ ॥
Siree Gurdayvay Nameh

I bow to the primal Guru.

I bow to the Truth that has existed throughout the ages.

I bow to True Wisdom.

I bow to the Great Divine Wisdom.

Protection: Invokes a light shield and stimulates
an alert mind to avoid accidents.

When Guru Ram Das wrote these words he bowed to Guru Amar Das, his True Guru and his father-in-law, and hailed Siri Guru Dev as the highest of the high, the Self-Existent, Eternal Truth. This mantra is proclaimed a mantra of protection. It is part of the Triple Mantra (as shown on the following page). Many people chant this mantra at any time when they might need extra protection. Recite this mantra before driving a car to delay yourself by nine seconds, so that you fail to show up on time for a fated accident. Yogi Bhajan also taught this mantra to be chanted, optionally, three times in a row after tuning in to a class with the Adi Mantra, providing a protective mind set. It is also often chanted three times at the beginning of a meeting to invoke the group protective mind and thwart potential volatility from misunderstanding.

"When you cannot be protected, this mantra shall protect you. When things stop, and won't move, this makes them move in your direction."

– Yogi Bhajan

© The Teachings of Yogi Bhajan, July 28, 1982

Aad Guray Nameh – Triple Mantra

ਆਦਿ ਗੁਰਏ ਨਮਹ॥
Aad Guray Nameh

ਜੁਗਾਦਿ ਗੁਰਏ ਨਮਹ॥
Jugaad Guray Nameh

ਸਤਿਗੁਰਏ ਨਮਹ॥
Sat Guray Nameh

ਸ੍ਰੀ ਗੁਰਦੇਵਏ ਨਮਹ॥
Siree Gurdayvay Nameh

ਆਦਿ ਸਚੁ ਜੁਗਾਦਿ ਸਚੁ॥ ਹੈ ਭੀ ਸਚੁ ਨਾਨਕ ਹੋਸੀ ਭੀ ਸਚੁ॥
Aad Sach Jugaad Sach Hai *Bhee* Sach Naanak Hosee *Bhee* Sach

ਆਦਿ ਸਚੁ ਜੁਗਾਦਿ ਸਚੁ॥ ਹੈ ਭਿ ਸਚੁ ਨਾਨਕ ਹੋਸੀ ਭਿ ਸਚੁ॥
Aad Sach Jugaad Sach Hai *Bhei* Sach Naanak Hosee *Bhei* Sach

I bow to the primal Guru.

I bow to the Truth that has existed throughout the ages.

I bow to True Wisdom.
I bow to the Great Divine Wisdom.

True in the beginning, True throughout the ages,
True even now, Nanak, Truth shall ever be.

True in the beginning, True throughout the ages,
True even now, Nanak, Truth shall ever be.

Protection: Clears psychic and physical obstacles in one's life.

This mantra is also known as the Triple Mantra. Chanting it clears obstacles and is a strong protector against car, plane, and other accidents. It cuts through opposing vibrations, thoughts, words, and actions. Chanting or listening to the Triple Mantra strengthens your magnetic field to deflect negativity. The first part of the mantra surrounds you with a powerful light shield of protection, the second part clears your spiritual path and the third part removes obstacles and blocks, allowing creative flow in your daily life.

Aap Sahaa-ee Hoaa

ਆਪ ਸਹਾਈ ਹੋਆ ਸੱਚੇ ਦਾ ਸੱਚਾ ਢੋਆ ਹਰਿ ਹਰਿ ਹਰਿ ॥
Aap sahaa-ee hoaa sachay daa sachaa doaa Har Har Har

You, Divine One, have become my refuge.
True is Your support, Great Creative Infinite.

Protection: To eliminate enemies and block the impact of animosity.

During your most difficult times, Guru comes to stand by you as your protector. Yogi Bhajan taught us that when chanted for 62 minutes during the ambrosial hours, this mantra can relieve unbearable financial pressure and give you mental self-control. This mantra meditation from the Siri Guru Granth Sahib is a gift to you that will let you penetrate the unknown without fear. It will give you protection and mental balance.

Gur Poorai Pooree Keetee

Guru Arjan Dev Ji
Raag Soorath
630

ਗੁਰਿ ਪੂਰੈ ਪੂਰੀ ਕੀਤੀ॥
Gur poorai pooree keetee

ਦੁਸਮਨ ਮਾਰਿ ਵਿਡਾਰੇ ਸਗਲੇ ਦਾਸ ਕਉ ਸੁਮਤਿ ਦੀਤੀ॥ ਰਹਾਉ॥
Dusaman maar vidaaray sagalay daas kao sumat deetee. || Rahaao

ਪ੍ਰਭਿ ਸਗਲੇ ਥਾਨ ਵਸਾਏ॥
Prabh sagalay thaan vasaa-ay

ਸੁਖਿ ਸਾਂਦ ਫਿਰਿ ਆਏ॥
Sukh saad fir aa-ay

The Perfect Guru is flawless and impeccable.

He has beaten and driven off my enemies,
and given me, His slave,
the sublime understanding of the neutral mind. | Pause

Protection: Opens up your own creative and protective energy.

This mantra invokes the Divine creative force to clear difficult situations in life and bring you safely through obstructions.

Hamaree Karo Haath Dai Rachhaa – from Benti Chaupai

Guru Gobind Singh Ji
Dasam Granth
1720

ਹਮਰੀ ਕਰੋ ਹਾਥ ਦੈ ਰੱਛਾ॥ ਪੂਰਨ ਹੋਇ ਚਿੱਤ ਕੀ ਇੱਛਾ॥

Hamaree karo haath dai rachhaa.
Pooran hoei chit kee eichhaa

ਤਵ ਚਰਨਨ ਮਨ ਰਹੈ ਹਮਾਰਾ॥ ਅਪਨਾ ਜਾਨ ਕਰੋ ਪ੍ਰਤਿਪਾਰਾ॥

Tav charnan man rehai hamaaraa.
Apnaa jaan karo pratipaaraa

ਹਮਰੇ ਦੁਸ਼ਟ ਸਭੈ ਤੁਮ ਘਾਵਹੁ॥ ਆਪੁ ਹਾਥ ਦੈ ਮੋਹਿ ਬਚਾਵਹੁ॥

Hamaray dusht sabhai tum ghaavaho.
Aap haath dai moeh bachaavaho

ਸੁਖੀ ਬਸੈ ਮੋਰੋ ਪਰਿਵਾਰਾ॥ ਸੇਵਕ ਸਿੱਖ ਸਭੈ ਕਰਤਾਰਾ॥

Sukhee basai moro parivaaraa.
Sayvak sikkhya sabhai kartaaraa

ਮੋ ਰੱਛਾ ਨਿਜ ਕਰ ਦੈ ਕਰਿਯੈ॥ ਸਭ ਬੈਰਨ ਕੌ ਆਜ ਸੰਘਰਿਯੈ॥

Mo rachhaa nij kar dai kariyai.
Sabh bairan kao aaj sanghariyai

ਪੂਰਨ ਹੋਇ ਹਮਾਰੀ ਆਸਾ॥ ਤੋਰਿ ਭਜਨ ਕੀ ਰਹੈ ਪਿਆਸਾ॥

Pooran ho-ei hamaaree aasaa.
Tor bhajan kee rehai piaasaa

May my mind focus on Your feet;
sustain me, as Your own.

Protect me, O Lord, with Your Hands;
may all my heart's desires be fulfilled.

O Lord, destroy all my enemies and
guard me with Your hands.

O Creator, may my family live in comfort,
along with all devotees and disciples.

Always shelter and protect me, O Lord,
and gather this day all my enemies.

May all my aspirations be fulfilled;
let my thirst for Your Name remain perpetual.

Protection: For protection in dire circumstances.

Eik Ardaas

Bhatt Bal
Swaiyay Mehl 5
1406

ਹਮ ਅਵਗੁਨਿ ਭਰੇ ਏਕੁ ਗੁਨੁ ਨਾਹੀ ਅੰਮ੍ਰਿਤੁ ਛਾਡਿ ਬਿਖੈ ਬਿਖੁ ਖਾਈ॥

**Ham avagun bharay ayk gun naahee
amrit chhaad bikhai bikh khaa-ee**

ਮਾਯਾ ਮੋਹ ਭਰਮ ਪੈ ਭੂਲੇ ਸੁਤ ਦਾਰਾ ਸਿਉ ਪ੍ਰੀਤਿ ਲਗਾਈ॥

**Maayaa moh bharam pai bhoolay
sut daaraa sio preet lagaa-ee**

ਇਕੁ ਉਤਮ ਪੰਥੁ ਸੁਨਿਓ ਗੁਰ ਸੰਗਤਿ ਤਿਹ ਮਿਲੰਤ ਜਮ ਤ੍ਰਾਸ ਮਿਟਾਈ॥

**Eik utam panth sunio gur sangat
teh milant jam traas mitaa-ee**

ਇਕ ਅਰਦਾਸਿ ਭਾਟ ਕੀਰਤਿ ਕੀ ਗੁਰ ਰਾਮਦਾਸ ਰਾਖਹੁ ਸਰਣਾਈ॥

**Eik ardaas bhaat keerat kee
Gur Raam Daas raakho sarnaa-ee**

I am without virtue, I have not even one virtue.
I turned away from nectar and ate poison.

Lost in doubt and temptation,
I slept, in love with the world and maya.

I have heard that the most exalted path of all
is the Sadh Sangat.
Joining it, the fear of death is taken away.

This one prayer of Keerat the poet is
that Guru Ram Das ever surround me with
His Divine protection.
Keep me sheltered from falsehood and
maya in His sanctuary.

Protection: Brings you to a protected state of
purity and grace.

This shabad is a prayer to become humble and
to connect you with the protective kindness of
Guru Ram Das.

Kirtan Sohilaa

ਸੋਹਿਲਾ ਰਾਗੁ ਗਉੜੀ ਦੀਪਕੀ ਮਹਲਾ ੧

Sohilaa raag gauree deepakee mehalaa pehlaa

ੴ ਸਤਿਗੁਰ ਪ੍ਰਸਾਦਿ॥

Ik ong kaar satigur prasaad

ਜੈ ਘਰਿ ਕੀਰਤਿ ਆਖੀਐ ਕਰਤੇ ਕਾ ਹੋਇ ਬੀਚਾਰੋ॥

Jai ghar keerat aakhee-ai kartay kaa ho-ei beechaaro

ਤਿਤੁ ਘਰਿ ਗਾਵਹੁ ਸੋਹਿਲਾ ਸਿਵਰਿਹੁ ਸਿਰਜਨਹਾਰੋ॥

Tit ghar gaavaho sohilaa sivaraho sirjanahaaro

ਤੁਮ ਗਾਵਹੁ ਮੇਰੇ ਨਿਰਭਉ ਕਾ ਸੋਹਿਲਾ॥

Tum gaavaho mayray nirbhau kaa sohilaa

ਹਉ ਵਾਰੀ ਜਿਤੁ ਸੋਹਿਲੈ ਸਦਾ ਸੁਖੁ ਹੋਇ॥ 1 ॥ ਰਹਾਉ॥

Hau vaaree jit sohilai sadaa sukh ho-ei. Rahaao

ਨਿਤ ਨਿਤ ਜੀਅੜੇ ਸਮਾਲੀਅਨਿ ਦੇਖੈਗਾ ਦੇਵਣਹਾਰੁ॥

Nit nit jeearay samaalee-an daykhaigaa dayvanahaar

ਤੇਰੇ ਦਾਨੈ ਕੀਮਤਿ ਨਾ ਪਵੈ ਤਿਸੁ ਦਾਤੇ ਕਵਨੁ ਸੁਮਾਰੁ ॥

Tayray daanai keemat naa pavai tis daatay kavan sumaar

ਸੰਬਤਿ ਸਾਹਾ ਲਿਖਿਆ ਮਿਲਿ ਕਰਿ ਪਾਵਹੁ ਤੇਲੁ ॥

Sambat saahaa likhiaa mil kar paavaho tayl

ਦੇਹੁ ਸਜਨ ਅਸੀਸੜੀਆ ਜਿਉ ਹੋਵੈ ਸਾਹਿਬ ਸਿਉ ਮੇਲੁ ॥

Dayho sajan aseesaree-aa jio hovai saahib sio mayl

ਘਰਿ ਘਰਿ ਏਹੋ ਪਾਹੁਚਾ ਸਦੜੇ ਨਿਤ ਪਵੰਨਿ ॥

Ghar ghar ayho paahuchaa sadaray nit pavann

ਸਦਣਹਾਰਾ ਸਿਮਰੀਐ ਨਾਨਕ ਸੇ ਦਿਹ ਆਵੰਨਿ ॥

Sadanhaaraa simaree-ai naanak say dih aavann

ਰਾਗ ਆਸਾ ਮਹਲਾ ੧

Raag aasaa mehalaa pehlaa

ਛਿਅ ਘਰ ਛਿਅ ਗੁਰ ਛਿਅ ਉਪਦੇਸ ॥

Chhia ghar chhia gur chhia upadays

ਗੁਰੁ ਗੁਰੁ ਏਕੋ ਵੇਸ ਅਨੇਕ ॥

Gur gur ayko vays anayk

ਬਾਬਾ ਜੈ ਘਰਿ ਕਰਤੇ ਕੀਰਤਿ ਹੋਇ॥

Baabaa jai ghar kartay keerat ho-ei

ਸੋ ਘਰੁ ਰਾਖੁ ਵਡਾਈ ਤੋਇ॥ 1॥ ਰਹਾਉ॥

So ghar raakh vadaa-ee to-ei. Rahaao

ਵਿਸੁਏ ਚਸਿਆ ਘੜੀਆ ਪਹਰਾ ਥਿਤੀ ਵਾਰੀ ਮਾਹੁ ਹੋਆ॥

Visuay chasiaa gharhee-aa pehraa thitee vaaree maaho hoaa.

ਸੂਰਜੁ ਏਕੋ ਰੁਤਿ ਅਨੇਕ॥ ਨਾਨਕ ਕਰਤੇ ਕੇ ਕੇਤੇ ਵੇਸ॥

Sooraj ayko rut anayk. Naanak kartay kay katay vays

ਰਾਗ ਧਨਾਸਰੀ ਮਹਲਾ ੧

Raag dhanaasree mehalaa pehlaa

ਗਗਨ ਮੈ ਥਾਲੁ ਰਵਿ ਚੰਦੁ ਦੀਪਕ ਬਨੇ ਤਾਰਿਕਾ ਮੰਡਲ ਜਨਕ ਮੋਤੀ॥

Gagan mai thaal rav chand deepak banay
taarikaa mandal janak motee

ਧੂਪ ਮਲਆਨ ਲੋ ਪਵਣੁ ਚਵਰੋ ਕਰੇ ਸਗਲ ਬਨਰਾਇ ਫੂਲੰਤ ਜੋਤੀ॥

Dhoop malaan lo pavan chavaro karay
sagal banraa-ei foolant jotee

ਕੈਸੀ ਆਰਤੀ ਹੋਇ॥ ਭਵ ਖੰਡਨਾ ਤੇਰੀ ਆਰਤੀ॥

Kaisee aartee ho-ei. Bhav khandanaa tayree aartee

ਅਨਹਤਾ ਸਬਦ ਵਾਜੰਤ ਭੇਰੀ॥ ਰਹਾਉ॥

Anahataa shabad vaajant bhayree. Rahaao

ਸਹਸ ਤਵ ਨੈਨ ਨਨ ਨੈਨ ਹਹਿ ਤੋਹਿ ਕਉ ਸਹਸ ਮੂਰਤਿ ਨਨਾ ਏਕ ਤੋਹੀ॥

Sahas tav nain nan nain heh toeh kau
sahas moorat nanaa ayk tohee

ਸਹਸ ਪਦ ਬਿਮਲ ਨਨ ਏਕ ਪਦ ਗੰਧ ਬਿਨੁ ਸਹਸ ਤਵ ਗੰਧ ਇਵ ਚਲਤ ਮੋਹੀ॥

Sahas pad bimal nan ayk pad gandh bin sahas
tav gandh eiv chalat mohee

ਸਭ ਮਹਿ ਜੋਤਿ ਜੋਤਿ ਹੈ ਸੋਇ॥ ਤਿਸ ਦੈ ਚਾਨਣਿ ਸਭ ਮਹਿ ਚਾਨਣੁ ਹੋਇ॥

Sabh meh jot jot hai so-ei
Tis dai chaanan sabh meh chaanan ho-ei

ਗੁਰ ਸਾਖੀ ਜੋਤਿ ਪਰਗਟੁ ਹੋਇ॥ ਜੋ ਤਿਸੁ ਭਾਵੈ ਸੁ ਆਰਤੀ ਹੋਇ॥

Gur saakhee jot pargat ho-ei
Jo tis bhaavai so aartee ho-ei

ਹਰਿ ਚਰਣ ਕਵਲ ਮਕਰੰਦ ਲੋਭਿਤ ਮਨੋ ਅਨਦਿਨੋ ਮੋਹਿ ਆਹੀ ਪਿਆਸਾ॥

Har charan kaval mukrand lobhit mano
andino moeh aahee piaasaa

ਕ੍ਰਿਪਾ ਜਲੁ ਦੇਹਿ ਨਾਨਕ ਸਾਰਿੰਗ ਕਉ ਹੋਇ ਜਾ ਤੇ ਤੇਰੈ ਨਾਇ ਵਾਸਾ॥

Kirpaa jal day naanak saaring kau
ho-ei jaa tay tayrai naa-ei vaasaa

ਰਾਗ ਗਉੜੀ ਪੂਰਬੀ ਮਹਲਾ ੪

Raag gauree poorbee mehalaa chauthaa

ਕਾਮਿ ਕਰੋਧਿ ਨਗਰੁ ਬਹੁ ਭਰਿਆ ਮਿਲਿ ਸਾਧੂ ਖੰਡਲ ਖੰਡਾ ਹੇ॥

Kaam karodh nagar baho bhariaa mil
saadhoo khandal khandaa hay

ਪੂਰਬਿ ਲਿਖਤ ਲਿਖੇ ਗੁਰੁ ਪਾਇਆ ਮਨਿ ਹਰਿ ਲਿਵ ਮੰਡਲ ਮੰਡਾ ਹੇ॥

Poorab likhat likhay gur paaei-aa man
har liv mandal mandaa hay

ਕਰਿ ਸਾਧੂ ਅੰਜੁਲੀ ਪੁਨੁ ਵਡਾ ਹੇ॥ ਕਰਿ ਡੰਡਉਤ ਪੁਨੁ ਵਡਾ ਹੇ॥ ਰਹਾਉ॥

Kar saadhoo anjulee pun vadaa hay.
Kar dandaut pun vadaa hay. Rahaao

ਸਾਕਤ ਹਰਿ ਰਸ ਸਾਦੁ ਨ ਜਾਨਿਆ ਤਿਨ ਅੰਤਰਿ ਹਉਮੈ ਕੰਡਾ ਹੇ॥

Saakat har ras saad na jaaniaa tin
antar haumai kandaa hay

ਜਿਉ ਜਿਉ ਚਲਹਿ ਚੁਭੈ ਦੁਖੁ ਪਾਵਹਿ ਜਮਕਾਲੁ ਸਹਹਿ ਸਿਰਿ ਡੰਡਾ ਹੇ॥

Jio jio chaleh chubhai dukh paaveh
jamkaal seheh sir dandaa hay

ਹਰਿ ਜਨ ਹਰਿ ਹਰਿ ਨਾਮਿ ਸਮਾਨੇ ਦੁਖੁ ਜਨਮ ਮਰਣ ਭਵ ਖੰਡਾ ਹੇ॥

Har jan har har naam samaanay dukh
janam maran bhav khandaa hay

ਅਬਿਨਾਸੀ ਪੁਰਖੁ ਪਾਇਆ ਪਰਮੇਸਰੁ ਬਹੁ ਸੋਭ ਖੰਡ ਬ੍ਰਹਮੰਡਾ ਹੇ॥

Abinaasee purakh paaei-aa parmaysar baho
sobh khand brahmandaa hay

ਹਮ ਗਰੀਬ ਮਸਕੀਨ ਪ੍ਰਭ ਤੇਰੇ ਹਰਿ ਰਾਖੁ ਰਾਖੁ ਵਡ ਵਡਾ ਹੇ॥

Ham gareeb maskeen prabh tayray har
raakh raakh vad vadaa hay

ਜਨ ਨਾਨਕ ਨਾਮੁ ਅਧਾਰੁ ਟੇਕ ਹੈ ਹਰਿ ਨਾਮੇ ਹੀ ਸੁਖੁ ਮੰਡਾ ਹੇ॥

Jan naanak naam adhaar tayk hai har
naamay hee sukh mandaa hay

ਰਾਗੁ ਗਉੜੀ ਪੂਰਬੀ ਮਹਲਾ ॥ ੫

Raag gauree poorbee mehalaa panjvaa(n)

ਕਰਉ ਬੇਨੰਤੀ ਸੁਨਹੁ ਮੇਰੇ ਮੀਤਾ ਸੰਤ ਟਹਲ ਕੀ ਬੇਲਾ॥

Karau baynantee sunaho mayray
meetaa sant tahal kee baylaa

ਈਹਾ ਖਾਟਿ ਚਲਹੁ ਹਰਿ ਲਾਹਾ ਆਗੈ ਬਸਨੁ ਸੁਹੇਲਾ॥

Eehaa khaat chalaho har laahaa aagai basan suhaylaa

ਅਉਧ ਘਟੈ ਦਿਨਸੁ ਰੈਨਾਰੇ॥ਮਨ ਗੁਰ ਮਿਲਿ ਕਾਜ ਸਵਾਰੇ॥ ਰਹਾਉ॥

Audh ghatai dinas rainaaray. Man gur mil kaaj savaaray. Rahaao

ਇਹੁ ਸੰਸਾਰੁ ਬਿਕਾਰੁ ਸੰਸੇ ਮਹਿ ਤਰਿਓ ਬ੍ਰਹਮ ਗਿਆਨੀ॥

Eiho sansaar bikaar sansay meh tario braham giaanee

ਜਿਸਹਿ ਜਗਾਇ ਪੀਆਵੈ ਇਹੁ ਰਸੁ ਅਕਥ ਕਥਾ ਤਿਨਿ ਜਾਨੀ॥

Jiseh jagaa-ei pee-aavai eiho ras akath kathaa tin jaanee

ਜਾ ਕਉ ਆਏ ਸੋਈ ਬਿਹਾਝਹੁ ਹਰਿ ਗੁਰ ਤੇ ਮਨਹਿ ਬਸੇਰਾ॥

Jaa kau aa-ay soee bihaajhaho har gur tay maneh basayraa

ਨਿਜ ਘਰਿ ਮਹਲੁ ਪਾਵਹੁ ਸੁਖ ਸਹਜੇ ਬਹੁਰਿ ਨ ਹੋਇਗੋ ਫੇਰਾ॥

Nij ghar mehl paavaho sukh sahajay bahur na hoei-go fayraa

ਅੰਤਰਜਾਮੀ ਪੁਰਖ ਬਿਧਾਤੇ ਸਰਧਾ ਮਨ ਕੀ ਪੂਰੇ॥

Antarjaamee purakh bidhaatay sardhaa man kee pooray

ਨਾਨਕ ਦਾਸੁ ਇਹੈ ਸੁਖੁ ਮਾਗੈ ਮੋਕਉ ਕਰਿ ਸੰਤਨ ਕੀ ਧੂਰੇ॥

Naanak daas eihai sukh maagai
mokau kar santan kee dhooray

Sohilaa, the Song Of Praise.

Raag Gauree Deepakee, Mehalaa First Guru

In that house where holy ones
dwell on the praises of the One Lord,

in that house, sing songs of praise and
remember the Creator Lord.

Sing the songs of praise of my Fearless Lord.

I am a sacrifice to that song of praise
which brings eternal peace. Pause

Day after day, He cares for His beings;
the Great Giver watches over all.

Your gifts cannot be appraised;
how can anyone describe the Giver?

The day of marriage of the soul bride with her Lord has dawned.
Come, gather together and pour the oil over the threshold.

And give me all your blessings,
that I may know a perfect union with my Lord.

Unto each and every home,
into each and every heart,
this summons is sent;
the call comes each and every day.

Remember in meditation the One who summons us;
O Nanak, that day is drawing near!

Raag Aasa, Mehalaa First Guru

There are six schools of philosophy,
six teachers, and six sets of teachings.

But the Teacher of teachers is the One,
who appears in so many forms.

O Baba, that system in which the
praises of the Creator are sung,

follow that system; in it rests true greatness. Pause

The seconds, minutes, and hours,
days, weeks, and months,

And the various seasons originate from the one sun;

O Nanak, in just the same way,
the many forms originate from the Creator.

Raag Dhanaasaree Mehalaa First Guru

Upon that cosmic plate of the sky,
the sun and the moon are the lamps.
The stars and their orbs are the studded pearls.

The fragrance of sandalwood in the air is the temple incense,
and the wind is the fan.

All the plants of the world are the altar flowers in
offering to You, O Luminous Lord.

What a beautiful Aartee, lamplit worship service this is!

O Destroyer of Fear, this is Your Ceremony of Light.

The unstruck sound current of the Shabad is
the vibration of the temple drums.

You have thousands of eyes,
and yet You have no eyes.
You have thousands of forms,
and yet You do not have even one.

You have thousands of Lotus Feet,
and yet You do not have even one foot.
You have no nose, but You have thousands of noses.
This play of Yours entrances me.

Amongst all is the light.
You are that Light.

By this illumination,
that Light is radiant within all.

Through the Guru's teachings,
the Light shines forth.

That which is pleasing to Him is
the lamplit worship service.

My mind is enticed by the honeysweet
Lotus Feet of the Lord.
Day and night, I thirst for them.

Bestow the water of Your mercy upon Nanak,
the thirsty songbird, so that he may come to
dwell in Your Name.

Raag Gauree Poorbee Mehalaa Fourth Guru

The corporeal existence is filled to
overflowing with anger and sexual desire;
these were broken into bits when
I met with the Holy Saint.

By preordained destiny, I have met with the Guru.
I have entered into the realm of the Lord's love.

Greet the Holy Saint with your palms pressed together;
this is an act of great merit.

Bow down before Him;
this is a virtuous action indeed. Pause

The wicked shaaktas, the faithless cynics,
do not know the taste of the Lord's sublime essence.
The thorn of egotism is embedded deep within them.

The more they walk away, the deeper it pierces them,
and the more they suffer in pain. Until finally,
the Messenger of Death smashes his club against their heads.

The humble servants of the Lord are absorbed in
the Name of the Lord, Har, Har.

The pain of birth and the fear of death are eradicated.

They have found the Imperishable Supreme Being,
the Transcendent Lord God,
and they receive great honor throughout
all the worlds and realms.

I am poor and meek, O God, but I belong to You!
Save me, please save me, O Greatest of the Great!

Servant Nanak takes the sustenance and support of the Naam.
In the Name of the Lord, he enjoys celestial peace.

Raag Gauree Poorbee Mehalaa Fifth Guru

Listen, my friends, I beg of you.
Now is the time to serve the saints!

In this world, earn the profit of the Lord's Name,
and hereafter, you shall dwell in peace.
This life is diminishing, day and night.

Meeting with the Guru, your affairs shall be resolved.

This world is engrossed in corruption and cynicism.
Only those who know God are saved.

Only those who are awakened by the
Lord to drink in this sublime essence,
come to know the unspoken speech of the Lord.

Purchase only that for which you have come into the world,
and through the Guru, the Lord shall dwell within your mind.

Within the home of your own inner being,
you shall obtain the mansion of the
Lord's presence with intuitive ease.

You shall not be consigned again to the wheel of reincarnation.

O Inner Knower, Searcher of Hearts, O Primal Being,
Architect of Destiny: please fulfill this yearning of my mind.

Nanak, Your slave, begs for this happiness:
let me be the dust of the feet of the Saints.

Protection: Tunes you into the protection of the
Earth element and removes negativity from your
environment to give you peaceful, healing sleep.

This is the prayer recited at night by Sikhs before
sleeping. It is also recited following a death, and
before cremation. Guru Nanak, Guru Ram Das
and Guru Arjan contributed the five shabads
celebrating the bliss of union with the Divine and
lamenting the pain of separation. The first three
Shabads were uttered by Guru Nanak, the fourth
by Guru Ram Das and the fifth by Guru Arjan Dev.

Man Bilaas Bha-ay Saahib Kay

Guru Arjan Dev Ji
Raag Dhanasaree
682

ਮਨਿ ਬਿਲਾਸ ਭਏ ਸਾਹਿਬ ਕੇ ਅਚਰਜ ਦੇਖਿ ਬਡਾਈ॥
Man bilaas bhaay saahib kay acharaj daykh badaa-ee.

ਹਰਿ ਸਿਮਰਿ ਸਿਮਰਿ ਆਨਦ ਕਰਿ ਨਾਨਕ ਪ੍ਰਭਿ ਪੂਰਨ ਪੈਜ ਰਖਾਈ॥
Har simar simar aanad kar Naanak prabh pooran paij rakhaa-ee.

My mind is delighted, gazing upon the marvelous,
glorious greatness of the Master.

Remembering, remembering the Master in meditation,
Nanak is in ecstasy.
The Divine One in perfection has protected and
preserved my honor.

Protection: For protection and preservation of honor.

Naal Naraa-ein Mayrai Jamdoot

Guru Arjan Dev Ji
Raag Soorath
630

ਨਾਲਿ ਨਰਾਇਣੁ ਮੇਰੈ॥ ਜਮਦੂਤੁ ਨ ਆਵੈ ਨੇਰੈ॥
Naal naraa-ein mayrai. Jamdoot na aavai nayrai

The Lord is always with me.
The Messenger of Death does not approach me.

Protection: Creates a spiritual foundation that is
destruction-proof.

Na Sattrai, Na Mittrai

Guru Gobind Singh Ji
Jaap Sahib
Dasam Granth

ਨ ਸੱਤ੍ਰੈ॥ ਨ ਮਿੱਤ੍ਰੈ॥ ਨ ਭਰਮੰ॥ ਨ ਭਿੱਤ੍ਰੈ॥
Na sattrai. Na mittrai. Na bharmang. Na bhittrai.

ਨ ਕਰਮੰ॥ ਨ ਕਾਏ॥ ਅਜਨਮੰ॥ ਅਜਾਏ॥
Na karmang. Na kaa-ay. Ajunmang. Ajaa-ay.

ਨ ਚਿਤ੍ਰੈ॥ ਨ ਮਿੱਤ੍ਰੈ॥ ਪਰੇ ਹੈਂ॥ ਪਵਿੱਤ੍ਰੈ॥
Na chitrai. Na mittrai. Paray hai(n). Pavittrai.

ਪ੍ਰਿਥੀਸੈ॥ ਅਦੀਸੈ॥ ਅਦ੍ਰਿਸੈ॥ ਅਕ੍ਰਿਸੈ॥
Pritheesai. Adeesai. Adrisai. Akrisai

You have no enmity with anyone,
and also no friendship.
You also have no delusion or fear.

O Lord, You are neither subject to the
effect of Karma (Deeds),
nor do You take birth on that account.
You never take birth.
You were not born of a woman.

No one can draw Your picture.
You have no friend.
You remain aloof from the creation,
and are pure and perfect.

O Lord, You are the Master of the earth.
You are the Master right from the beginning.
You are invisible. You are never weakened.

Protection: Builds a shield of protection around you.

This mantra is from the *Dasam Granth* of the
Tenth Sikh Master, Guru Gobind Singh. It brings
an experience of inner confirmation of the true
reality, the Infinite within you.

Rakhay Rakhanahaar Aap Ubaarian

Guru Arjan Dev Ji
Raag Gurji
517

ਰਖੇ ਰਖਣਹਾਰਿ ਆਪਿ ਉਬਾਰਿਅਨੁ ॥
Rakhay rakhanahaar aap ubaarian

ਗੁਰ ਕੀ ਪੈਰੀ ਪਾਇ ਕਾਜ ਸਵਾਰਿਅਨੁ ॥
Gur kee pairee paa-ei kaaj savaarian

ਹੋਆ ਆਪਿ ਦਇਆਲੁ ਮਨਹੁ ਨ ਵਿਸਾਰਿਅਨੁ ॥
Hoaa aap dei-aal manaho na visaarian

ਸਾਧ ਜਨਾ ਕੈ ਸੰਗਿ ਭਵਜਲੁ ਤਾਰਿਅਨੁ ॥
Saadh janaa kai sang bhavajal taarian

ਸਾਕਤ ਨਿੰਦਕ ਦੁਸਟ ਖਿਨ ਮਾਹਿ ਬਿਦਾਰਿਅਨੁ ॥
Saakat nindak dusht khin maa-eh bidaarian

ਤਿਸੁ ਸਾਹਿਬ ਕੀ ਟੇਕ ਨਾਨਕ ਮਨੈ ਮਾਹਿ ॥
Tis saahib kee tayk naanak manai maa-eh

ਜਿਸੁ ਸਿਮਰਤ ਸੁਖੁ ਹੋਇ ਸਗਲੇ ਦੂਖ ਜਾਹਿ ॥
Jis simrat sukh ho-ei sagalay dookh jaa-eh

Mantra

Thou who savest, save us all and take us across,

uplifting and giving us the excellence.

You gave us the touch of the lotus feet of the Guru,
and all our jobs are done.

You have become merciful, kind, and compassionate;
and so our mind does not forget Thee.

In the company of the holy ones You
take us from misfortune and
calamities, scandals, and disrepute.

Godless, slanderous enemies—
You finish them in timelessness.

That great Lord is my anchor.

Nanak, keep firm in your mind.
By meditating and repeating His Name

all happiness comes and all sorrows and pain go away.

Protection: Invokes protection and adds energy and support to one's being.

This mantra is from the Siri Guru Granth Sahib. Rehiras is the evening prayer of the Sikhs that was written by Guru Arjan. Chanting this mantra helps when you are physically weak or have limited wealth. This is a victory song which allows us to be guided by God's graceful and merciful hand. It does away with the obstacles to fulfilling one's destiny. Chanting this mantra helps against fluctuations of the mind. This mantra is included in the Aquarian Sadhana and is done as a part of the daily practice in the morning meditations for Kundalini Yoga practitioners.

Raakh Lee-ay Tin Rakhanahaar

Guru Arjan Dev Ji
Raag Bilaval
819

ਰਾਖਿ ਲੀਏ ਤਿਨਿ ਰਖਨਹਾਰਿ ਸਭ ਬਿਆਧਿ ਮਿਟਾਈ॥
Raakh lee-ay tin rakhanahaar sabh bi-aadh mitaa-ee

ਕਹੁ ਨਾਨਕ ਕਿਰਪਾ ਭਈ ਪ੍ਰਭ ਭਏ ਸਹਾਈ॥
Kaho Naanak kirpaa bha-ee prabh bha-ay sahaa-ee

The Savior Lord has saved me,
and eradicated all my sickness.

Says Nanak, God has showered me with His mercy;
He has become my help and support.

Protection: Brings protection from illness.

Ridh Sidh Ghar Mo Sabh Ho-ee

Guru Gobind Singh Ji
Dasam Granth
1723

ਰਿੱਧਿ ਸਿੱਧਿ ਘਰ ਮੋ ਸਭ ਹੋਈ॥
Ridh sidh ghar mo sabh ho-ee

ਦੁਸ਼ਟ ਛਾਹ ਛ੍ਵੈ ਸਕੈ ਨ ਕੋਈ॥
Dusht chaah chhavai sakai na ko-ee

Miracles descend at their homes and in their minds and
they receive Divine blessings.

Evil persons cannot go near even
the shadows of these persons.

Protection: To surround yourself with a golden
shield of protective light.

Simar Simar Simar Sukh Paaei-aa

Guru Arjan Dev Ji
Raag Bilaval
824

ਸਿਮਰਿ ਸਿਮਰਿ ਸਿਮਰਿ ਸੁਖੁ ਪਾਇਆ ਚਰਨ ਕਮਲ ਰਖੁ ਮਨ ਮਾਹੀ॥
Simar simar simar sukh paaei-aa charan kamal rakh man maahee

Meditating, meditating,
meditating in remembrance,
I have found peace;
I have enshrined
His Lotus Feet within my mind.

Protection: Keeps your environments secure in a
protected realm.

Taatee Vaao Na Laga-ee

Guru Arjan Dev Ji
Raag Bilaval
819

ਤਾਤੀ ਵਾਉ ਨ ਲਗਈ ਪਾਰਬ੍ਰਹਮ ਸਰਣਾਈ॥

Taatee vaao na laga-ee paarabrahm sarnaa-ee

ਚਉਗਿਰਦ ਹਮਾਰੈ ਰਾਮ ਕਾਰ ਦੁਖੁ ਲਗੈ ਨ ਭਾਈ॥

Chaugirad hamaarai raam kaar dukh lagai na bhaa-ee

The hot wind does not even touch one who is
under the protection of the Supreme Almighty One.

On all four sides I am surrounded by the
circle of protection of
the Divine One. And pain does not afflict me,
O Siblings of Destiny.

Protection: For protection from all of life's hardships.

Tant Mant Nah Joha-ee

Guru Arjan Dev Ji
Raag Bilaaval

818

ਤੰਤੁ ਮੰਤੁ ਨਹ ਜੋਹਈ ਤਿਤੁ ਚਾਖੁ ਨ ਲਾਗੈ॥
Tant mant nah joha-ee tit chaakh na laagai.

He is not affected by charms and spells,
nor is he harmed by the evil eye.

Protection: Creates a protective shield in your auric body.

Teerath Tap Daei-aa Dat Daan

Guru Nanak Dev Ji
Japji Sahib
4

ਤੀਰਥੁ ਤਪੁ ਦਇਆ ਦਤੁ ਦਾਨੁ ॥
Teerath tap daei-aa dat daan

ਜੇ ਕੋ ਪਾਵੈ ਤਿਲ ਕਾ ਮਾਨੁ ॥
Jay ko paavai til kaa maan

ਸੁਣਿਆ ਮੰਨਿਆ ਮਨਿ ਕੀਤਾ ਭਾਉ ॥
Suni-aa manni-aa man keetaa bhaa-o

ਅੰਤਰਗਤਿ ਤੀਰਥਿ ਮਲਿ ਨਾਉ ॥
Antargat teerath mal naao

ਸਭਿ ਗੁਣ ਤੇਰੇ ਮੈ ਨਾਹੀ ਕੋਇ ॥
Sabh gun tayray mai naahee ko-ei

ਵਿਣੁ ਗੁਣ ਕੀਤੇ ਭਗਤਿ ਨ ਹੋਇ ॥
Vin gun keetay bhagat na ho-ei

ਸੁਅਸਤਿ ਆਥਿ ਬਾਣੀ ਬਰਮਾਉ ॥
Suasat aath baanee barmaa-o

ਸਤਿ ਸੁਹਾਣੁ ਸਦਾ ਮਨਿ ਚਾਉ॥

Sat suhaan sadaa man chaa-o

ਕਵਣੁ ਸੁ ਵੇਲਾ ਵਖਤੁ ਕਵਣੁ ਕਵਣ ਥਿਤਿ ਕਵਣੁ ਵਾਰੁ॥

Kavan su vaylaa vakhat kavan, kavan thit kavan vaar

ਕਵਣਿ ਸਿ ਰੁਤੀ ਮਾਹੁ ਕਵਣੁ ਜਿਤੁ ਹੋਆ ਆਕਾਰੁ॥

Kavan si rutee maaho kavan jit hoaa aakaar

ਵੇਲ ਨ ਪਾਈਆ ਪੰਡਤੀ ਜਿ ਹੋਵੈ ਲੇਖੁ ਪੁਰਾਣੁ॥

Vayl na paaee-aa pandatee, ji hovai laykh puraan

ਵਖਤੁ ਨ ਪਾਇਓ ਕਾਦੀਆ ਜਿ ਲਿਖਨਿ ਲੇਖੁ ਕੁਰਾਣੁ॥

Vakhat na paa-ei-o kaadee-aa, ji likhan laykh kuraan

ਥਿਤਿ ਵਾਰੁ ਨਾ ਜੋਗੀ ਜਾਣੈ ਰੁਤਿ ਮਾਹੁ ਨਾ ਕੋਈ॥

Thit vaar naa jogee jaanai rut maaho naa koee

ਜਾ ਕਰਤਾ ਸਿਰਠੀ ਕਉ ਸਾਜੇ ਆਪੇ ਜਾਣੈ ਸੋਈ॥

Jaa kartaa sirthee kau saajay, aapay jaanai soee

ਕਿਵ ਕਰਿ ਆਖਾ ਕਿ ਸਾਲਾਹੀ ਕਿਉ ਵਰਨੀ ਕਿਵ ਜਾਣਾ॥

Kiv kar aakhaa kiv saalaahee, kio varnee kiv jaanaa

ਨਾਨਕ ਆਖਣਿ ਸਭੁ ਕੋ ਆਖੈ ਇਕਦੂ ਇਕੁ ਸਿਆਣਾ॥

Naanak aakhan sabh ko aakhai, eikdoo eik siaanaa

ਵਡਾ ਸਾਹਿਬੁ ਵਡੀ ਨਾਈ ਕੀਤਾ ਜਾ ਕਾ ਹੋਵੈ॥

Vadaa saahib vadee naa-ee, keetaa jaa kaa hovai

ਨਾਨਕ ਜੇ ਕੋ ਆਪੌ ਜਾਣੈ ਅਗੈ ਗਇਆ ਨ ਸੋਹੈ॥

Naanak jay kao aapao jaanai, agai gaei-aa na sohai

Pilgrimages, austerities, compassion, and charity,

by themselves bring only an iota of merit.

Listening, accepting with humility and love in your mind,

cleanse yourself at the sacred shrine deep within your being.

All virtues are Yours, O Lord; l have none at all.

Without virtue, there is no devotional worship.

l bow unto the Lord of the world;

to His word, to Brahma, the Creator.

God is true and beautiful; His mind is forever joyful.

What was that time, and what was that moment?

What was that day, and what was that date?

What was that season, and what was that month,
when the universe was created?

The pandits, the religious scholars, cannot find that time,

even if it is written in the Puraanas.

That time is not known to the Qazis,
who study the Koran.

The day and date are not known to the yogis,

nor is the month or the season.

The Creator who fashioned this creation –
He alone knows.

How can we speak of Him?
How can we praise Him?

How can we describe Him?
How can we know Him?

O Nanak, everyone speaks of Him,
each more clever than the others.

Great is the Master, Great is His Name.

Whatever happens is by His will.

O Nanak, one who claims to know everything,

Shall not be decorated in the world hereafter.

From the *Siri Guru Granth Sahib*, the 21st pauree of
Japji Sahib, Guru Nanak Dev Ji.

Protection: Maintains your status, grace, and position.

Self-Esteem

Apunaa Naam Aapay Dee-aa

Guru Arjan Dev Ji
Raag Sorath
623

ਅਪੁਨਾ ਨਾਮੁ ਆਪੇ ਦੀਆ
Apunaa naam aapay dee-aa

ਪ੍ਰਭ ਕਰਨਹਾਰ ਰਖਿ ਲੀਆ ॥
Prabh karanhaar rakh lee-aa

The Creator bestows the Name.

The Creator protects and saves us.

Self-esteem: To infuse self-esteem and recognition of your self-worth.

Birthee Kaday Na Hova-ee

Guru Arjan Dev Ji
Raag Bilaaval
819

ਬਿਰਥੀ ਕਦੇ ਨ ਹੋਵਈ ਜਨ ਕੀ ਅਰਦਾਸਿ॥
Birthee kaday na hova-ee jan kee ardaas

ਨਾਨਕ ਜੋਰੁ ਗੋਵਿੰਦ ਕਾ ਪੂਰਨ ਗੁਣਤਾਸਿ॥
Naanak jor govind kaa pooran guntaas

The prayer of the Lord's humble servant is
never offered in vain.

Nanak receives the strength of the
Perfect Lord of the Universe, the treasure of excellence.

Self-esteem: Builds self-esteem and inner confidence.

Ghar Baahar Tayraa Bharvaasaa

Guru Arjan Dev Ji
Raag Dhanaasree
677

ਘਰਿ ਬਾਹਰਿ ਤੇਰਾ ਭਰਵਾਸਾ ਤੂ ਜਨ ਕੈ ਹੈ ਸੰਗਿ॥
Ghar baahar tayraa bharvaasaa too jan kai hai sang.

At home, and outside, I place my trust in You;
You are always with Your humble servant.

Self-esteem: Takes away insecurities.

Gobinday Mukanday Udaaray Apaaray
Haree-ang Karee-ang Nirnaamay Akaamay

Guru Gobind Singh ji
Jap Sahib
Dasam Granth page 14

ਗੋਬਿੰਦੇ॥ ਮੁਕੰਦੇ॥ ਉਦਾਰੇ॥ ਅਪਾਰੇ॥
Gobinday. Mukanday. Udaaray. Apaaray.

ਹਰੀਅੰ॥ ਕਰੀਅੰ॥ ਨ੍ਰਿਨਾਮੇ॥ ਅਕਾਮੇ॥
Hareeang. Karee-ang. Nirnaamay. Akaamay.

Sustainer, Liberator, Enlightener, Infinite

Destroyer, Creator, Nameless, Desireless

Self-esteem: Breaks through and clears
deep-seated blocks in the subconscious mind and
rebuilds your confidence and self-esteem.

Besides helping to cleanse the subconscious mind,
this mantra balances the hemispheres of the brain,
bringing compassion and patience.

Gur Poorai Mayree Raakh La-ee

Guru Arjan Dev Ji
Raag Bilaaval
823

ਗੁਰਿ ਪੂਰੈ ਮੇਰੀ ਰਾਖਿ ਲਈ॥
Gur poorai mayree raakh la-ee

ਅੰਮ੍ਰਿਤ ਨਾਮੁ ਰਿਦੇ ਮਹਿ ਦੀਨੋ ਜਨਮ ਜਨਮ ਕੀ ਮੈਲੁ ਗਈ॥
Amrit naam riday meh deeno janam janam kee mail ga-ee

The Perfect Guru has saved me.

He has enshrined the ambrosial Name of the Lord within my heart,
and the filth of countless incarnations has been washed away.

Self-esteem: Instills self-confidence and self-esteem.

Har Har Har Har Haree Haree

Har Haree is found in several places in the
Siri Guru Granth Sahib, including
Guru Arjan Dev Ji
Raag Gauree
191

ਹਰਿ ਹਰਿ ਹਰਿ ਹਰਿ ਹਰੀ ਹਰੀ॥
Har Har Har Har Haree Haree

Har Haree – Creative Infinity

Self-Esteem: Builds a deep sense of self-reliance.

This mantra allows you to separate your identity
from your success. It gives you potency, productiv-
ity, and caliber. It makes you experience and believe
in yourself. Then success comes to serve you,
rather than you running after it. The entire mantra
is repeated on a single breath. The tone is a relaxed
monotone that varies in emphasis automatically as
you proceed through the stages of the mantra. Each
'Har' is one beat and each 'Hari' is 2 beats. This meditation was taught by Guru Nanak. It was passed on
by Baba Siri Chand and later, by Guru Hargobind.

Hay Gobind

Guru Arjan Dev Ji
Raag Malaar
1273

ਹੇ ਗੋਬਿੰਦ ਹੇ ਗੋਪਾਲ ਹੇ ਦਇਆਲ ਲਾਲ ॥ 1 ॥ ਰਹਾਉ ॥
Hay gobind hay gopaal hay daei-aal laal. Rahaao

ਪ੍ਰਾਨ ਨਾਥ ਅਨਾਥ ਸਖੇ ਦੀਨ ਦਰਦ ਨਿਵਾਰ ॥
Praan naath anaath sakhay deen darad nivaar.

ਹੇ ਸਮੂਥ ਅਗਮ ਪੂਰਨ ਮੋਹਿ ਮਇਆ ਧਾਰਿ ॥
Hay samrath agam pooran moeh maei-aa dhaar.

ਅੰਧ ਕੂਪ ਮਹਾ ਭਇਆਨ ਨਾਨਕ ਪਾਰਿ ਉਤਾਰ ॥
Andh koop mahaa bhaei-aan naanak paar utaar.

O Lord of the Universe, O Lord of the world,
O dear merciful Beloved.

You are the Master of the breath of life,
the Companion of the lost and forsaken,
the Destroyer of the pains of the poor.

O all-powerful, inaccessible, perfect Lord,
please shower me with Your mercy.

Please, carry Nanak across the terrible,
deep dark pit of the world to the other side.

From the *Siri Guru Granth Sahib*, Guru Arjan Dev Ji

Self-esteem: Eliminates fear and insecurity and
builds confidence in achievement and expansion of self.

Jis Neech Ko Koee Na Jaanai

Guru Arjan Dev Ji
Raag Aasaa
386

ਜਿਸੁ ਨੀਚ ਕਉ ਕੋਈ ਨ ਜਾਨੈ॥
Jis neech ko koee na jaanai

ਨਾਮੁ ਜਪਤ ਉਹੁ ਚਹੁ ਕੁੰਟ ਮਾਨੈ॥
Naam japat oh chau kunt maanai

ਦਰਸਨ ਮਾਗਉ ਦੇਹਿ ਪਿਆਰੇ॥
Darshan maago dayh piaaray

ਤੁਮਰੀ ਸੇਵਾ ਕਉਨ ਕਉਨ ਨ ਤਾਰੇ॥ ਰਹਾਉ॥
Tumree sayvaa koun koun na taaray || Rahaao

ਜਾ ਕੈ ਨਿਕਟਿ ਨ ਆਵੈ ਕੋਈ॥
Jaa kai nikat na aavai ko-ee

ਸਗਲ ਸ੍ਰਿਸਟਿ ਉਆ ਕੈ ਚਰਨ ਮਲਿ ਧੋਈ॥
Sagal srist oo-aa kai charan mal dho-ee

ਜੋ ਪ੍ਰਾਨੀ ਕਾਹੂ ਨ ਆਵਤ ਕਾਮ ॥
Jo praanee kaahoo na aavat kaam

ਸੰਤ ਪ੍ਰਸਾਦਿ ਤਾ ਕੋ ਜਪੀਐ ਨਾਮ ॥
Sant prasaad taa ko japee-ai naam

ਸਾਧਸੰਗਿ ਮਨ ਸੋਵਤ ਜਾਗੇ ॥
Saadhsang man sovat jaagay

ਤਬ ਪ੍ਰਭ ਨਾਨਕ ਮੀਠੇ ਲਾਗੇ ॥
Tab prabh naanak meethay laagay

Even a wretched human who
committed vile past deeds,

chanting the Naam, the Name of the Lord,
that one is honored in the four directions.

I beg for the blessed vision of the Master's Darshan;
please, grant it to me.

O Beloved! Serving You — who has not been saved? Pause

That person, whom no one wanted to be near,
now the whole world comes to wash the dirt of his feet.

That mortal, who is of no use to anyone at all,
by the Grace of the Saints, meditates on the Naam.

In the Saadh Sangat, the Company of the Holy,

the sleeping mind awakens.

Then, O Nanak, God seems sweet.

From the Siri Guru Granth, Guru Arjan Dev Ji

Self-esteem: Purifies the ego and brings self-esteem.

Kaval Nain Madhur Bain

Bhatt Gayandh
Svaiyay Mehl 5
1402

ਕਵਲ ਨੈਨ ਮਧੁਰ ਬੈਨ ਕੋਟਿ ਸੈਨ ਸੰਗ ਸੋਭ
Kaval nain madhur bain kot sain sang sobh

ਕਹਤ ਮਾ ਜਸੋਦ ਜਿਸਹਿ ਦਹੀ ਭਾਤੁ ਖਾਹਿ ਜੀਉ॥
Kahat maa jasod jiseh dahee bhaat khaa-eh jeeo

ਦੇਖਿ ਰੂਪੁ ਅਤਿ ਅਨੂਪੁ ਮੋਹ ਮਹਾ ਮਗ ਭਈ
Daykh roop at anoop moh mahaa mag bhaa-ee

ਕਿੰਕਨੀ ਸਬਦ ਝਨਤਕਾਰ ਖੇਲੁ ਪਾਹਿ ਜੀਉ॥
Kinkanee shabad jhanatkaar khayl paa-eh jeeo

ਕਾਲ ਕਲਮ ਹੁਕਮੁ ਹਾਥਿ ਕਹਹੁ ਕਉਨੁ ਮੇਟਿ ਸਕੈ
Kaal kalam hukam haath kahaho kaun mayt sakai

ਈਸੁ ਬਮੁ ਗ੍ਯ੍ਯਾਨੁ ਧ੍ਯ੍ਯਾਨੁ ਧਰਤ ਹੀਐ ਚਾਹਿ ਜੀਉ॥
Ees bamm gyaan dhyaan dharat hee-ai chaa-eh jeeo

ਸਤਿ ਸਾਚੁ ਸ੍ਰੀ ਨਿਵਾਸੁ ਆਦਿ ਪੁਰਖੁ ਸਦਾ ਤੁਹੀ
Sat saach siree nivaas aad purakh sadaa tuhee

ਵਾਹਿਗੁਰੂ ਵਾਹਿਗੁਰੂ ਵਾਹਿਗੁਰੂ ਵਾਹਿ ਜੀਉ ॥

Whaa-hay Guroo, Whaa-hay Guroo, Whaa-hay Guroo, Whaa-hay Jeeo

You are blessed with the Lord's Name,
the supreme mansion, and clear understanding.

You are the Formless, Infinite Lord;
who can compare to You?

For the sake of the purehearted devotee Prahlaad,

You took the form of the Man-lion,
to tear apart and destroy Harnaakhash with your claws.

You are the Infinite Supreme Lord God;
with your symbols of power,
You deceived Baliraja; who can know You?

You are forever true, the home of excellence,
the Primal Supreme Being.

Whaa-hay Guroo, Whaa-hay Guroo, Whaa-hay Guroo, Whaa-hay Jeeo.

Self-Esteem: Brings high self-esteem, courage,
and excellence.

Paarbrahm Karay Pratipaalaa

Guru Arjan Dev Ji
Raag Sorath
623

ਪਾਰਬ੍ਰਹਮੁ ਕਰੇ ਪ੍ਰਤਿਪਾਲਾ ॥
Paarbrahm karay pratipaalaa

ਸਦ ਜੀਅ ਸੰਗਿ ਰਖਵਾਲਾ ॥
Sad jeea sang rakhavaalaa

The Supreme Lord God cherishes and nurtures me.

The Supreme One is always with me and
is the protector of my soul.

Self-esteem: Increases self-confidence and self-love.

Paarbrahm Nibaahee Pooree

Guru Arjan Dev Ji
Raag Sorath
623

ਪਾਰਬ੍ਰਹਮਿ ਨਿਬਾਹੀ ਪੂਰੀ
Paarbrahm nibaahee pooree

ਕਾਈ ਬਾਤ ਨ ਰਹੀਆ ਊਰੀ॥
Kaa-ee baat na rahee-aa ooree

The Supreme Master has stood by me and fulfilled me

and nothing is left unfinished.

Self-esteem: To know your Divine worth.

Patit Puneet Kar Leenay

Guru Arjan Dev Ji
Raag Sorath
623

ਪਤਿਤ ਪੁਨੀਤ ਕਰਿ ਲੀਨੇ ॥
Patit puneet kar leenay

ਕਰਿ ਕਿਰਪਾ ਹਰਿ ਜਸੁ ਦੀਨੇ ॥
Kar kirpaa har jas deenay.

I have many offences,
but the Divine Creator has made me pure.

The Merciful One has blessed me with
songs of praise for the Divine.

Self-esteem: Invokes creative flow to reverse
a negative self-image.

Sat Naam Whaa-hay Guroo

ਸਤਿ ਨਾਮ ਵਾਹਿ ਗੁਰੂ
Sat Naam Whaa-hay Guroo

True is my identity. Great is the Guru,
the Divine Teacher who brings us
from darkness to light.

Self-esteem: Uplifts you and builds your
self-confidence and self-esteem.

This mantra strengthens the entire lower triangle
and gives you the power to transform fear into
love.

Sat Saach Siree Nivaas

Bhatt Gayandh
Svaiyay Mehl 5
1402

ਸਤਿ ਸਾਚੁ ਸ੍ਰੀ ਨਿਵਾਸੁ ਆਦਿ ਪੁਰਖੁ ਸਦਾ ਤੁਹੀ
Sat saach siree nivaas aad purakh sadaa tuhee

ਵਾਹਿਗੁਰੂ ਵਾਹਿਗੁਰੂ ਵਾਹਿਗੁਰੂ ਵਾਹਿ ਜੀਉ ॥
Whaa-hay Guroo, Whaa-hay Guroo, Whaa-hay Guroo, Whaa-hay Jeeo

You are forever True,
the Home of Excellence,
the Primal Supreme Being.
Whaa-hay Guru, Whaa-hay Guru,
Whaa-hay Guru, Whaa-hay Jeeo.

Self-esteem: To build self-confidence and
awareness of inner wisdom.

NOTE: This is from the same shabd as page 237:
Kaval Nain Madhur Bain.

Sayvak Kao Nikatee Ho-ei Dikhaavai

Guru Arjan Dev Ji
Raag Aasaa
403

ਸੇਵਕ ਕਉ ਨਿਕਟੀ ਹੋਇ ਦਿਖਾਵੈ॥

Sayvak kao nikatee ho-ei dikhaavai.

ਜੋ ਜੋ ਕਹੈ ਠਾਕੁਰ ਪਹਿ ਸੇਵਕੁ ਤਤਕਾਲ ਹੋਇ ਆਵੈ॥

Jo jo kahai thaakur pa-eh sayvak tatkaal ho-ei aavai

The Lord appears near at hand to the servant.
Whatever the servant asks of the Lord and
Master immediately comes to pass.

Self-esteem: To bring self-identity, honor and distinction.

Vich Kartaa Purakh Khalo-aa

Guru Arjan Dev Ji
Raag Sorath
623

ਵਿਚਿ ਕਰਤਾ ਪੁਰਖੁ ਖਲੋਆ ॥
Vich kartaa purakh khalo-aa

ਵਾਲੁ ਨ ਵਿੰਗਾ ਹੋਆ ॥
Vaal na vingaa ho-aa

ਮਜਨੁ ਗੁਰ ਆਂਦਾ ਰਾਸੇ ॥
Majan gur aandaa raasay

ਜਪਿ ਹਰਿ ਹਰਿ ਕਿਲਵਿਖ ਨਾਸੇ ॥
Jap har har kilavikh naasay

The Creator Lord Himself stood between us,

And not a hair upon my head was touched.

The Guru made my cleansing bath successful.

Meditating on the Lord Har, Har, my sins were erased.

Self-esteem: Removes insecurity and uncertainty.

Self-Realization

Gagan Mai Thaal Rav
Chand Deepak Banay

Guru Nanak Dev Ji
Raag Dhanaasree
663

ਗਗਨ ਮੈ ਥਾਲੁ ਰਵਿ ਚੰਦੁ ਦੀਪਕ ਬਨੇ ਤਾਰਿਕਾ ਮੰਡਲ ਜਨਕ ਮੋਤੀ॥

Gagan mai thaal rav chand deepak banay
taarikaa mandal janak motee

ਧੂਪੁ ਮਲਆਨਲੋ ਪਵਣੁ ਚਵਰੋ ਕਰੇ ਸਗਲ ਬਨਰਾਇ ਫੁਲੰਤ ਜੋਤੀ॥

Dhoop malaanalo pavan chavaro karay sagal
banaraa-ei foolant jotee

ਕੈਸੀ ਆਰਤੀ ਹੋਇ ਭਵ ਖੰਡਨਾ ਤੇਰੀ ਆਰਤੀ॥

Kaisee aartee ho-ei. Bhav khandanaa tayree aartee

ਅਨਹਤਾ ਸਬਦ ਵਾਜੰਤ ਭੇਰੀ॥ 1॥ ਰਹਾਉ॥

Anahataa shabad vaajant bhayree. Rahaao

ਸਹਸ ਤਵ ਨੈਨ ਨਨ ਨੈਨ ਹਹਿ ਤੋਹਿ ਕਉ ਸਹਸ ਮੂਰਤਿ ਨਨਾ ਏਕ ਤੋਹੀ॥

Sahas tav nain nan nain heh toeh kau
sahas moorat nanaa ayk tohee

ਸਹਸ ਪਦ ਬਿਮਲ ਨਨ ਏਕ ਪਦ ਗੰਧ ਬਿਨੁ ਸਹਸ ਤਵ ਗੰਧ ਇਵ ਚਲਤ ਮੋਹੀ॥

Sahas pad bimal nan ayk pad, gandh bin sahas
tav gandh eiv chalat mohee

ਸਭ ਮਹਿ ਜੋਤਿ ਜੋਤਿ ਹੈ ਸੋਇ॥ ਤਿਸ ਦੈ ਚਾਨਣਿ ਸਭ ਮਹਿ ਚਾਨਣੁ ਹੋਇ॥

Sabh meh jot jot hai so-ei. Tis dai chaanan sabh maeh chaanan ho-ei

ਗੁਰ ਸਾਖੀ ਜੋਤਿ ਪਰਗਟੁ ਹੋਇ॥ ਜੋ ਤਿਸੁ ਭਾਵੈ ਸੁ ਆਰਤੀ ਹੋਇ॥

Gur saakhee jot pargat ho-ei. Jo tis bhaavai so aartee ho-ei

ਹਰਿ ਚਰਣ ਕਵਲ ਮਕਰੰਦ ਲੋਭਿਤ ਮਨੋ ਅਨਦਿਨੋ ਮੋਹਿ ਆਹੀ ਪਿਆਸਾ॥

Har charan kaval makarand lobhit mano
Anadino moeh aahee piaasaa

ਕ੍ਰਿਪਾ ਜਲੁ ਦੇਹਿ ਨਾਨਕ ਸਾਰਿੰਗ ਕਉ ਹੋਇ ਜਾ ਤੇ ਤੇਰੈ ਨਾਮਿ ਵਾਸਾ॥

Kirpaa jal dayh naanak saaring kau ho-ei jaa tay tayrai naa-ei vaasaa.

Upon that cosmic plate of the sky,
the sun and the moon are the lamps.
The stars and their orbs are the studded pearls.

The fragrance of sandalwood in the air is the temple incense,
and the wind is the fan.

All the plants of the world are the altar flowers in
offering to You, O Luminous Lord.

Mantra

What a beautiful Aartee, lamplit worship service this is!

O Destroyer of Fear, this is Your Ceremony of Light.

The unstruck sound current of the Shabad is
the vibration of the temple drums.

You have thousands of eyes, and yet You have no eyes.
You have thousands of forms, and yet You do not have even one.

You have thousands of Lotus Feet,
and yet You do not have even one foot.

You have no nose, but You have thousands of noses.
This play of Yours entrances me.

Amongst all is the Light. You are that Light.

By this illumination, that Light is radiant within all.

Through the Guru's teachings, the Light shines forth.

That which is pleasing to Him is the lamplit worship service.

My mind is enticed by the honeysweet Lotus Feet of the Lord.
Day and night, I thirst for them.

Bestow the water of Your mercy upon Nanak,
the thirsty songbird, so that he may come to
dwell in Your Name.

Self-Realization: Awakens the beauty of your
soul, so that we may dwell in peace and love.

This shabad is written by Guru Nanak, in praise
of the Creator and all of the creation. It is part
of Kirtan Sohilaa, a prayer recited at bedtime by
Sikhs.

Gurdayv Maataa Gurdayv Pitaa

Guru Arjan Dev Ji
Raag Gauree
250 and 262 at the beginning and
at the end of the "52 Letters"

ਗੁਰਦੇਵ ਮਾਤਾ ਗੁਰਦੇਵ ਪਿਤਾ ਗੁਰਦੇਵ ਸੁਆਮੀ ਪਰਮੇਸੁਰਾ॥
Gurdayv maataa gurdayv pitaa gurdayv suaamee paramaysuraa

ਗੁਰਦੇਵ ਸਖਾ ਅਗਿਆਨ ਭੰਜਨੁ ਗੁਰਦੇਵ ਬੰਧਿਪ ਸਹੋਦਰਾ॥
Gurdayv sakhaa agiaan bhanjan gurdayv bandhip sahodaraa

ਗੁਰਦੇਵ ਦਾਤਾ ਹਰਿ ਨਾਮੁ ਉਪਦੇਸੈ ਗੁਰਦੇਵ ਮੰਤੁ ਨਿਰੋਧਰਾ॥
Gurdayv daataa har naam updaysai gurdayv mant nirodharaa

ਗੁਰਦੇਵ ਸਾਂਤਿ ਸਤਿ ਬੁਧਿ ਮੂਰਤਿ ਗੁਰਦੇਵ ਪਾਰਸ ਪਰਸ ਪਰਾ॥
Gurdayv saant sat budh moorat gurdayv paaras paras paraa

ਗੁਰਦੇਵ ਤੀਰਥੁ ਅੰਮ੍ਰਿਤ ਸਰੋਵਰੁ ਗੁਰ ਗਿਆਨ ਮਜਨੁ ਅਪਰੰਪਰਾ॥
Gurdayv teerath amrit sarovar gur giaan majan aparanparaa

ਗੁਰਦੇਵ ਕਰਤਾ ਸਭਿ ਪਾਪ ਹਰਤਾ ਗੁਰਦੇਵ ਪਤਿਤ ਪਵਿਤ ਕਰਾ॥
Gurdayv kartaa sabh paap hartaa gurdayv patit pavit karaa

ਗੁਰਦੇਵ ਆਦਿ ਜੁਗਾਦਿ ਜੁਗੁ ਜੁਗੁ ਗੁਰਦੇਵ ਮੰਤੁ ਹਰਿ ਜਪਿ ਉਧਰਾ ॥
Gurdayv aad jugaad jug jug gurdayv mant har jap udharaa

ਗੁਰਦੇਵ ਸੰਗਤਿ ਪ੍ਰਭ ਮੇਲਿ ਕਰਿ ਕਿਰਪਾ ਹਮ ਮੂੜ ਪਾਪੀ ਜਿਤੁ ਲਗਿ ਤਰਾ ॥
Gurdayv sangat prabh mayl kar kirpaa hum moor paapee jit lag taraa

ਗੁਰਦੇਵ ਸਤਿਗੁਰੁ ਪਾਰਬ੍ਰਹਮੁ ਪਰਮੇਸਰੁ ਗੁਰਦੇਵ ਨਾਨਕ ਹਰਿ ਨਮਸਕਰਾ ॥
Gurdayv satgur parabrahm parmaysar gurdayv
Naanak har namaskaraa

Divine Guru is my mother,
Divine Guru is my father;

Divine Guru is my transcendent Lord and Master.

Divine Guru is my companion,
the destroyer of ignorance;
Divine Guru is my relative and brother.

Divine Guru is the Giver,
the Teacher of the Lord's Name.

Divine Guru is the mantra which never fails.

Divine Guru is the image of peace, truth, and wisdom.
Divine Guru is the Philosopher's Stone –
touching it, one is transformed.

Divine Guru is the sacred shrine of pilgrimage,
and the pool of divine ambrosia;
bathing in the Guru's Wisdom,
one experiences the Infinite.

Divine Guru is the Creator,
and the destroyer of all sins;
Divine Guru is the purifier of sinners.

Divine Guru existed at the primal beginning,
throughout the ages, in each and every age.
Divine Guru is the mantra of the Lord's Name;
chanting it, one is saved.

O God, please be merciful to me,
that I may be with the Divine Guru;
I am a foolish sinner, but holding on to Him,
I am carried across.

Divine Guru is the True Guru,
the supreme Lord God, the transcendent Lord;
Nanak bows in humble reverence to the Lord,
the Divine Guru.

Self-Realization: Takes you to your true reality
and an experience of Godliness.

Har Har Har Har Hareenaam

ਹਰਿ ਹਰਿ ਹਰਿ ਹਰਿ ਹਰੀਨਾਮ॥

Har Har Har Har Hareenaam

Har	Infinite Creative One.
Hareenaam	Manifestation of the Infinite One in action, the blessing chain.

Self-Realization: Aligns your conscious mind with the song of your soul.

Har Jee Har Har

ਹਰਿ ਜੀ ਹਰਿ ਹਰਿ
Har Jee Har Har

ਹਰਿ ਹਰਿ ਹਰਿ ਜੀ
Har Har Har Jee

Har – Creative flow of the universe

Jee – Soul

Self-Realization: Brings realization of one's destiny.

Kiaa Savanaa Kiaa Jaagnaa
Gurmukh Tay Parvaan

Guru Raam Daas Ji
Gauree ki vaar Mehla 4
312–313

ਕਿਆ ਸਵਣਾ ਕਿਆ ਜਾਗਣਾ ਗੁਰਮੁਖਿ ਤੇ ਪਰਵਾਣੁ॥
Kiaa savanaa kiaa jaaganaa gurmukh tay parvaan

ਜਿਨਾ ਸਾਸਿ ਗਿਰਾਸਿ ਨ ਵਿਸਰੈ ਸੇ ਪੂਰੇ ਪੁਰਖ ਪਰਧਾਨ॥
Jinaa saas giraas na visarai say pooray purakh pardhaan

ਕਰਮੀ ਸਤਿਗੁਰੁ ਪਾਈਐ ਅਨਦਿਨੁ ਲਗੈ ਧਿਆਨੁ॥
Karmee satgur paaee-ai anadin lagai dhiaan

ਤਿਨ ਕੀ ਸੰਗਤਿ ਮਿਲਿ ਰਹਾ ਦਰਗਹ ਪਾਈ ਮਾਨੁ॥
Tin kee sangat mil rahaa dargeh paa-ee maan

ਸਉਦੇ ਵਾਹੁ ਵਾਹੁ ਉਚਰਹਿ ਉਠਦੇ ਭੀ ਵਾਹੁ ਕਰੇਨਿ॥
Sauday vaaho vaahio uchareh uthday bhee vaaho karayn

ਨਾਨਕ ਤੇ ਮੁਖ ਉਜਲੇ ਜਿ ਨਿਤ ਉਠਿ ਸੰਮਾਲੇਨਿ॥
Naanak tay mukh ujalay jih nit uth samaalayn

Who is asleep, and who is awake?
Those who are Gurmukh are approved.

Those who do not forget the Lord,
with each and every breath and morsel of food,

are the perfect and famous persons.

By His Grace they find the True Guru;
night and day, they meditate.

I join the society of those persons, and in so doing,

I am honored in the Court of the Lord.

While asleep, they chant, "Whaa-ho! Whaa-ho!", and

while awake, they chant, "Whaa-ho!" as well.

O Nanak, radiant are the faces of those,

who rise up early each day, and dwell upon the Lord.

From the *Siri Guru Granth Sahib*, Guru Ram Das.

Self-Realization: Brings majesty of self and the
experience of realization through sadhana.

Man Jeetai Jag Jeet

Guru Nanak Dev Ji
Japji Sahib
6

ਮਨਿ ਜੀਤੈ ਜਗੁ ਜੀਤੁ ॥

Man jeetai jag jeet

Conquer your mind and you conquer the world.

Self-Realization: Brings serenity and stability to all of your environments, home, work, and relationships.

Naanak Chintaa Mat Karo

Guru Angad Dev Ji
Raag Raamkalee
955

ਨਾਨਕ ਚਿੰਤਾ ਮਤਿ ਕਰਹੁ ਚਿੰਤਾ ਤਿਸ ਹੀ ਹੋਇ॥
Naanak chintaa mat karo chintaa tis hee hay-ei.

O Nanak, don't be anxious; the Lord will take care of you.

Self-Realization: To rid one of ego and bring true self-identity.

Ray Man Eih Bidh Jog Kamaa-o

Guru Gobind Singh
Raag Ramkalee
Dasam Granth
1344

ਰੇ ਮਨ ਇਹ ਬਿਧਿ ਜੋਗੁ ਕਮਾਓ॥
Ray man eih bidh jog kamaa-o.

ਸਿੰਙੀ ਸਾਚ ਅਕਪਟ ਕੰਠਲਾ
Singee saach akapat kanthalaa

ਧਿਆਨ ਬਿਭੂਤ ਚੜ੍ਹਾਓ॥
Dhiaan bibhoot charhaao.

ਤਾਤੀ ਗਹੁ ਆਤਮ ਬਸਿ ਕਰ ਕੀ
Taatee gaho aatam bas kar kee

ਭਿੱਛਾ ਨਾਮ ਅਧਾਰੰ॥
Bhichhaa naam adhaarang.

ਬਾਜੇ ਪਰਮ ਤਾਰ ਤਤੁ ਹਰਿ ਕੋ
Baajay param taar tat har ko

ਉਪਜੈ ਰਾਗ ਰਸਾਰੰ॥
Upajai raag rasaarang.

ਉਘਟੈ ਤਾਨ ਤਰੰਗ ਰੰਗਿ

Ughatai taan tarang rang.

ਅਤਿ ਗਿਆਨ ਗੀਤ ਬੰਧਾਨੰ॥

At gyaan geet bandhaanang.

ਚਕਿ ਚਕਿ ਰਹੇ ਦੇਵ ਦਾਨਵ ਮੁਨਿ

Chak chak rehay dayv daanav mun

ਛਕਿ ਛਕਿ ਬਯੋਮ ਬਿਵਾਨੰ॥

Chhak chhak bayom bivaanang.

ਆਤਮ ਉਪਦੇਸ ਭੇਸੁ ਸੰਜਮ ਕੌ

Aatam upadays bhays sanjam ko

ਜਾਪ ਸੁ ਅਜਪਾ ਜਾਪੈ॥

Jaap so ajapaa jaapai.

ਸਦਾ ਰਹੈ ਕੰਚਨ ਸੀ ਕਾਯਾ

Sadaa rehai kanchan see kaayaa

ਕਾਲ ਨ ਕਬਹੂੰ ਬਯਾਪੈ॥

Kaal na kabahoo bayaapai.

Oh my mind, practice Yoga in this way.

Let Truth be your horn, sincerity your necklace, and

meditation the ashes you apply on your body.

Make self-control your stringed instrument.

Let the soul (self) be the alms bowl in
which you collect the sweet Naam and this will be
the only support you ever need.

The universe plays its divine music.

The sound of reality is shrill, but this is where God is.

When you listen to the reality from
this place of awareness the
sweet essence of Raag arises.

Waves of melodies, emotions,
and passions arise and flow through you.
Bind yourself with the song of God.

The universe spins like a potter's wheel and
from it fly demons and angels.

The sage listens to this and instead of
getting caught in either one,
the sage drinks in the nectar of the heavens and is
carried to the heavens in a divine chariot.

Instruct and clothe yourself with self-control.

Meditate unto Infinity until you are
meditating without meditating.

In this way, your body shall remain forever golden,

and Death shall never approach you.

Self-Realization: Brings you wisdom, the purity of
a yogi, and recognition of your Divine essence.

Perfection of this shabad can make you like a
Golden Buddha. For everyone who believes in
higher values, recite this shabad in perfect sound. It
is a very perfect combination. As a shabad you can
sing it 11 times a day, and you will feel the miraculous
effect of it on your body, mind, and soul.

This shabad comes from the Dasam Granth of
Guru Gobind Singh. His entire bani is meant to
penetrate through the mental body, right into your
own spirit. The secret of this bani is that it is a
pure Naad Yoga in the Brij Baashaa language. The
combination and permutation of sound is totally
practical in this bani. The tongue creates a pressure
on the upper palate. This shabad has the capacity
to awaken one from being bewitched by incurable
disease. If sung properly through the tongue and
mouth, it can bring total health. Each sound must
be said exactly correctly. It can lead to a perfect
state of mental health and surrounding spirit.

Sat Naam

ਸਤਿਨਾਮ
Sat Naam

Sat means truth, the reality of one's existence.

Naam means name, or identity.

This mantra is often translated as "Truth is my identity", "Truth is God's Name" or "True is the Name."

Self-Realization: Awakens the soul and gives you your destiny.

This mantra affirms our existence in truth and it is used widely by Kundalini Yogis around the world as a greeting or to preface or close a communication. Sat Naam is a Beej mantra, or seed mantra, and represents the primal seed of truth from which the whole creation has sprouted. Within the seed is contained all the knowledge of the fully grown tree. The essence or seed is the identity of truth embodied in condensed form.This mantra balances the five tattvas (elements) of the universe.

The one who becomes absorbed in Sat Naam merges into the Light of Truth within the self. Everything else is temporary — our family will depart, our houses will crumble, and we will also leave our body behind. Everything around us is ever-changing except for Sat Nam. The Divine Truth is forever constant and stable.

Too(n) Bhaaro Suaamee Mayraa

Guru Arjan Dev Ji
Raag Sorath
629

ਤੂੰ ਭਾਰੋ ਸੁਆਮੀ ਮੇਰਾ ॥
Too(n) bhaaro suaamee mayraa

ਸੰਤਾਂ ਭਰਵਾਸਾ ਤੇਰਾ ॥
Santaa(n) bharavaasaa tayraa

ਨਾਨਕ ਪ੍ਰਭ ਸਰਨਾਈ ॥
Naanak prabh sarnaa-ee

ਮੁਖਿ ਨਿੰਦਕ ਕੈ ਛਾਈ ॥
Mukh nindak kai chhaa-ee

You are my Great Lord and Master.

You are the support of the saints.

Nanak has entered God's Sanctuary.

The faces of the slanderers are blackened with ashes.

Self-Realization: To find the Divine light and your ultimate sanctuary within.

Whaa-hay Guroo Gurmantra Hai

ਵਾਹਿਗੁਰੂ ਗੁਰਮੰਤ੍ਰੂ ਹੈ ਜਪਿ ਹਉਮੈ ਖੋਈ
Whaa-hay Guroo Gurmantra hai jap haumai khoee

Wahe Guru is the Guru mantra. By reciting it the ego is eradicated and we are filled with bliss and virtue.

Self-Realization: Brings inner purification, self-radiance and bliss.

Stability

Dandaut Bandan Anik Baar

Guru Arjan Dev Ji
Raag Gauree
256

ਡੰਡਉਤਿ ਬੰਦਨ ਅਨਿਕ ਬਾਰ ਸਰਬ ਕਲਾ ਸਮਰਥ ॥
Dandaut bandan anik baar sarab kalaa samrath.

ਡੋਲਨ ਤੇ ਰਾਖਹੁ ਪ੍ਰਭੂ ਨਾਨਕ ਦੇ ਕਰਿ ਹਥ ॥
Dolan tay raakho prabhoo Naanak day kar hath.

I bow down and fall to the ground in humble adoration
countless times to the Supreme Master,
who possesses all powers.

Please protect me and save me from wandering,
Great Master. Reach out and give Nanak your hand.

Stability: To gain stability and courage to
meet your destiny.

Dharam Khand

Guru Nanak Dev Ji
Japji Sahib
7

ਧਰਮ ਖੰਡ ਕਾ ਏਹੋ ਧਰਮੁ॥

Dharam khand kaa ayho dharam

ਗਿਆਨ ਖੰਡ ਕਾ ਆਖਹੁ ਕਰਮੁ॥

Giaan khand kaa aakh-ho karam

ਕੇਤੇ ਪਵਣ ਪਾਣੀ ਵੈਸੰਤਰ ਕੇਤੇ ਕਾਨ ਮਹੇਸ॥

Kaytay pavan paanee vaisantar kaytay kaan mahays

ਕੇਤੇ ਬਰਮੇ ਘਾੜਤਿ ਘੜੀਅਹਿ ਰੂਪ ਰੰਗ ਕੇ ਵੇਸ॥

Kaytay barmay ghaarat gharee-eh roop rang kay vays

ਕੇਤੀਆ ਕਰਮ ਭੂਮੀ ਮੇਰ ਕੇਤੇ ਕੇਤੇ ਧੂ ਉਪਦੇਸ॥

Kaytee-aa karam bhoomee mayr kaytay kaytay dhoo upadays

ਕੇਤੇ ਇੰਦ ਚੰਦ ਸੂਰ ਕੇਤੇ ਕੇਤੇ ਮੰਡਲ ਦੇਸ॥

Kaytay eind chand soor kaytay kaytay mandal days

ਕੇਤੇ ਸਿਧ ਬੁਧ ਨਾਥ ਕੇਤੇ ਕੇਤੇ ਦੇਵੀ ਵੇਸ ॥

Kaytay sidh budh naath kaytay kaytay dayvee vays

ਕੇਤੇ ਦੇਵ ਦਾਨਵ ਮੁਨਿ ਕੇਤੇ ਕੇਤੇ ਰਤਨ ਸਮੁੰਦ ॥

Kaytay dayv daanav mun kaytay kaytay ratan samund

ਕੇਤੀਆ ਖਾਣੀ ਕੇਤੀਆ ਬਾਣੀ ਕੇਤੇ ਪਾਤ ਨਰਿੰਦ ॥

Kaytee-aa khaanee kaytee-aa baanee kaytay paat narind

ਕੇਤੀਆ ਸੁਰਤੀ ਸੇਵਕ ਕੇਤੇ ਨਾਨਕ ਅੰਤੁ ਨ ਅੰਤੁ ॥

Kaytee-aa surtee sayvak kaytay Naanak ant na ant

This is righteous living in the realm of Dharma.

And now we speak of the realm of spiritual wisdom.

So many winds, waters, and fires; so many Krishnas and Shivas.

So many Brahmas, fashioning forms of great beauty,

adorned and dressed in so many colors.

So many worlds and lands for working out karma.

So many lessons to be learned!

So many Indras, so many moons and suns,
so many planets and countries.

So many siddhas, so many buddhas, and yoga masters.

So many goddesses of various kinds.

So many demigods, so many demons and silent sages.

So many oceans of jewels.

So many ways of life, so many languages.

So many dynasties of rulers.

So many intuitives, so many selfless servants.

O Nanak, there is no end, no limit.

From the *Siri Guru Granth Sahib*, the 35th pauree of
Japji Sahib, by Guru Nanak Dev Ji.

Stability: Gives you the breadth to do your duty
and fulfill your responsibility.

Eik Ong Kaar

Guru Nanak Dev Ji
Japji Sahib
Page 1

ਇਕ ਓਅੰਕਾਰ
Eik Ong Kaar

There is One Creator of the creation,
and One Spirit moves throughout all creation.

Stability: Brings stability.

Hukamee Hovan Aakaar

Guru Nanak Dev Ji
Japji Sahib
SGGS page 1

ਹੁਕਮੀ ਹੋਵਨਿ ਆਕਾਰ ਹੁਕਮੁ ਨ ਕਹਿਆ ਜਾਈ॥
Hukamee hovan aakaar hukam na kahi-aa jaa-ee.

ਹੁਕਮੀ ਹੋਵਨਿ ਜੀਅ ਹੁਕਮਿ ਮਿਲੈ ਵਡਿਆਈ॥
Hukamee hovan jeea hukam milai vadiaa-ee.

ਹੁਕਮੀ ਉਤਮੁ ਨੀਚੁ ਹੁਕਮਿ ਲਿਖਿ ਦੁਖ ਸੁਖ ਪਾਈਅਹਿ॥
Hukamee utam neech hukam likh dukh sukh paaee-eh.

ਇਕਨਾ ਹੁਕਮੀ ਬਖਸੀਸ ਇਕਿ ਹੁਕਮੀ ਸਦਾ ਭਵਾਈਅਹਿ॥
Eiknaa hukamee bakhsheesh eik hukamee sadaa bhavaaee-eh.

ਹੁਕਮੈ ਅੰਦਰਿ ਸਭੁ ਕੋ ਬਾਹਰਿ ਹੁਕਮ ਨ ਕੋਇ॥
Hukamai andar sabh ko baahar hukam na ko-ei.

ਨਾਨਕ ਹੁਕਮੈ ਜੇ ਬੁਝੈ ਤ ਹਉਮੈ ਕਹੈ ਨ ਕੋਇ॥
Naanak hukamai jay bujhai ta haumai kahai na ko-ei.

By His command, bodies come into being.

His command cannot be described.

By His command, souls come into being.

By His command, glory and greatness are obtained.

By His command, some are high and some are low.

By His written command, pain and pleasure are obtained.

Some, by His command, are blessed and forgiven.

Others, by His command, wander aimlessly forever.

All are subject to His command.

No one is beyond His command.

O Nanak, one who understands His command,

does not speak in ego.

From the *Siri Guru Granth Sahib*, the second pauree of
Japji Sahib, Guru Nanak Dev Ji.

Stability: Imparts patience and stability.

Raatee Rutee Thitee Vaar

Guru Nanak Dev Ji
Japji Sahib
SGGS page 7

ਰਾਤੀ ਰੁਤੀ ਥਿਤੀ ਵਾਰ॥
Raatee rutee thitee vaar

ਪਵਣ ਪਾਣੀ ਅਗਨੀ ਪਾਤਾਲ॥
Pavan paanee aganee paataal

ਤਿਸੁ ਵਿਚਿ ਧਰਤੀ ਥਾਪਿ ਰਖੀ ਧਰਮ ਸਾਲ॥
Tis vich dhartee thaap rakhee dharam saal

ਤਿਸੁ ਵਿਚਿ ਜੀਅ ਜੁਗਤਿ ਕੇ ਰੰਗ॥
Tis vich jeea jugat kay rang

ਤਿਨ ਕੇ ਨਾਮ ਅਨੇਕ ਅਨੰਤ॥
Tin kay naam anayk anant

ਕਰਮੀ ਕਰਮੀ ਹੋਇ ਵੀਚਾਰੁ॥
Karmee karmee ho-ei veechaar

ਸਚਾ ਆਪਿ ਸਚਾ ਦਰਬਾਰੁ ॥

Sachaa aap sachaa darbaar

ਤਿਥੈ ਸੋਹਨਿ ਪੰਚ ਪਰਵਾਣੁ ॥

Tithai sohan panch parvaan

ਨਦਰੀ ਕਰਮਿ ਪਵੈ ਨੀਸਾਣੁ ॥

Nadaree karam pavai neeshaan

ਕਚ ਪਕਾਈ ਓਥੈ ਪਾਇ ॥

Kach pakaa-ee othai paa-ei

ਨਾਨਕ ਗਇਆ ਜਾਪੈ ਜਾਇ ॥

Naanak gei-aa jaapai jaa-ei

Days, nights, weeks, and seasons;

wind, water, fire, and nether regions;

in the midst of these
He established the Earth as a home for Dharma,
for righteous living.

Upon it, He placed the various species of beings.

Their names are uncounted and endless.

By their deeds and their actions, they shall be judged.

God Himself is True, and True is His court.

There, in perfect grace and ease, sit the self-elect,
the self-realized saints.

They receive the mark of grace from the Merciful Lord.

The ripe and the unripe, the good and the bad,
shall there be judged.

O Nanak, when you go home you shall see this.

From the *Siri Guru Granth Sahib* 34th pauree of Japji Sahib,
Guru Nanak Dev Ji.

Stability: Brings stability.

Surrender & Devotion

Aap Gavaaee-ai Taa Soh Paaee-ai

Guru Nanak Dev Ji
Raag Tilang
722

ਆਪੁ ਗਵਾਈਐ ਤਾ ਸਹੁ ਪਾਈਐ ਅਉਰੁ ਕੈਸੀ ਚਤੁਰਾਈ ॥
Aap gavaaee-ai taa soh paaee-ai aur kaisee chaturaa-ee

Give up your self, and so obtain your Beloved Lord.
What clever tricks are of any use?

Surrender: Gives you the power to surrender your
ego to your Infinite Divine Being.

Dithay Sabhay Thaav

Guru Arjan Dev Ji
Phunhay Fifth Mehl
1362

ਡਿਠੇ ਸਭੇ ਥਾਵ ਨਹੀ ਤੁਧੁ ਜੇਹਿਆ॥
Dithay sabhay thaav nahee tudh jayhi-aa

ਬਧੋਹੁ ਪੁਰਖਿ ਬਿਧਾਤੈ ਤਾਂ ਤੂ ਸੋਹਿਆ॥
Badhaho purakh bidhaatai taa(n) too sohi-aa

ਵਸਦੀ ਸਘਨ ਅਪਾਰ ਅਨੂਪ ਰਾਮਦਾਸ ਪੁਰ॥
Vasadee saghan apaar anoop RaamDaas pur

ਹਰਿਹਾਂ ਨਾਨਕ ਕਸਮਲ ਜਾਹਿ ਨਾਇਐ ਰਾਮਦਾਸ ਸਰ॥
Harihaa(n) Naanak kasamal jaa-eh naaei-ai RaamDaas sar

I have seen all places, but none compares to You.

The Primal Creator, Architect of Destiny,
has established You.

Thus You are adorned and embellished.
The place of Ram Das is prosperous and full of life,
and incomparably beautiful. O Creator!
Bathing in the Sacred Pool of Raam Daas,
(Nectar Tank at the Golden Temple in Amritsar)
the sins are washed away, O Nanak.

Devotion: Gives you a devotional experience in the House of Guru Ram Das.

This mantra connects you directly to the consciousness of Guru Ram Das.

Kaytiaa Dookh Bhookh Sad Maar

Guru Nanak Dev Ji
Japji Sahib
SGGS page 5

ਕੇਤਿਆ ਦੂਖ ਭੂਖ ਸਦ ਮਾਰ ॥
Kaytiaa dookh bhookh sad maar

ਏਹਿ ਭਿ ਦਾਤਿ ਤੇਰੀ ਦਾਤਾਰ ॥
Ayeh bhi daat tayree daataar

So many endure distress, deprivation, and constant abuse.

Even these are Your gifts, O Great Giver!

Surrender: Experience the gift of surrender to receive infinite return.

Ko Banjaaro Raam Ko Mayraa

Bhagat Ravi Daas Ji
Raag Gauree
345–346

ਕੋ ਬਨਜਾਰੋ ਰਾਮ ਕੋ ਮੇਰਾ
Ko banjaaro raam ko mayraa

ਘਟ ਅਵਘਟ ਡੂਗਰ ਘਣਾ ਇਕੁ ਨਿਰਗੁਣੁ ਬੈਲੁ ਹਮਾਰ॥
Ghat avaghat dhoogar ghanaa eik nirgun bail hamaar

ਰਮਈਏ ਸਿਉ ਇਕ ਬੇਨਤੀ ਮੇਰੀ ਪੂੰਜੀ ਰਾਖੁ ਮੁਰਾਰਿ॥
Ramee-ay sio eik bayntee mayree poonjee raakh muraar

ਕੋ ਬਨਜਾਰੋ ਰਾਮ ਕੋ ਮੇਰਾ ਟਾਂਡਾ ਲਾਦਿਆ ਜਾਇ ਰੇ॥ ਰਹਾਉ॥
Ko banjaaro raam ko mayraa taandaa laadi-aa jaa-ei ray. Rahaao

ਹਉ ਬਨਜਾਰੋ ਰਾਮ ਕੋ ਸਹਜ ਕਰਉ ਬੁਾਪਾਰੁ॥
Hao banjaaro raam ko sahaj karao byaapaar

ਮੈ ਰਾਮ ਨਾਮ ਧਨੁ ਲਾਦਿਆ ਬਿਖੁ ਲਾਦੀ ਸੰਸਾਰਿ॥
Mai raam naam dhan laadi-aa bikh laadee sansaar

ਉਰਵਾਰ ਪਾਰ ਕੇ ਦਾਨੀਆ ਲਿਖਿ ਲੇਹੁ ਆਲ ਪਤਾਲੁ ॥

Urvaar paar kay daanee-aa likh layho aalpataal

ਮੋਹਿ ਜਮ ਡੰਡੁ ਨ ਲਾਗਈ ਤਜੀਲੇ ਸਰਬ ਜੰਜਾਲ ॥

Moeh jam dand na laaga-ee tajeelay sarab janjaal

ਜੈਸਾ ਰੰਗੁ ਕਸੁੰਭ ਕਾ ਤੈਸਾ ਇਹੁ ਸੰਸਾਰੁ ॥

Jaisaa rang kasumbh kaa taisaa eiho sansaar

ਮੇਰੇ ਰਮਈਏ ਰੰਗੁ ਮਜੀਠ ਕਾ ਕਹੁ ਰਵਿਦਾਸ ਚਮਾਰ ॥

Mayray ramee-ay rang majeeth kaa kaho RaviDaas chamaar

The path to God is very treacherous and mountainous.

All I have is this worthless ox.

I offer this one prayer to the Lord,
to preserve my capital.

Is there any merchant of the Lord to join me?
My cargo is loaded, and now I am leaving.
I am the merchant of the Lord; I deal in spiritual wisdom.

I have loaded the wealth of the Lord's Name;
the world has loaded poison.

O you who know this world and the world beyond,
write whatever nonsense you please about me.

The club of the Messenger of Death shall not strike me,
since I have cast off all entanglements.

Love of this world is like the pale,
temporary color of the safflower.

The color of my Lord's love,
however, is permanent,
like the dye of the madder plant.
So says Ravi Daas, the tanner.

Surrender: Releases one from worldly attachments
and brings realization of the Divine Name.

Trust

Aad Ant Aykai Avtaaraa

Guru Gobind Singh ji
Bente Chaupai
Dasam Granth page 1466

ਆਦਿ ਅੰਤਿ ਏਕੈ ਅਵਤਾਰਾ ॥
Aad ant aykai avtaaraa

ਸੋਈ ਗੁਰੁ ਸਮਝਿਜਹੁ ਹਮਾਰਾ ॥
Soee Guroo samjhi-ya-ho hamaaraa

The One who is the primal being,
from the beginning through all time —

Understand: that Divine Master is my Guru.

Trust: To gain the trust of others.

Jalay Hai Thalay Hai(n)

Guru Gobind Singh ji
Jaap Sahib
Dasam Granth Page 3

ਜਲੇ ਹੈਂ ॥ ਥਲੇ ਹੈਂ ॥ ਅਭੀਤ ਹੈਂ ॥ ਅਭੇ ਹੈਂ ॥
Jalay hai(n). Thalay hai(n). Abheet hai(n). Abhay hai(n).

ਪ੍ਰਭੂ ਹੈਂ ॥ ਅਜੂ ਹੈਂ ॥ ਅਦੇਸ ਹੈਂ ॥ ਅਭੇਸ ਹੈਂ ॥
Prabhoo hai(n). Ajoo hai(n). Adays hai(n). Abhays hai(n).

O Lord, You are present in water and land.
You are fearless and unfathomable.

You are the Master of all. You are Immutable.
You do not belong to any one country or
have any particular costume to wear.

From the *Dasam Granth* of the Tenth Master,
Guru Gobind Singh Ji.

Trust: Brings trust in relationships and takes away
personality conflicts.

Union

Aad Pooran Madh Pooran

Guru Arjan Dev Ji
Raag Jaithsree
705

ਆਦਿ ਪੂਰਨ ਮਧਿ ਪੂਰਨ
Aad pooran madh pooran

ਅੰਤਿ ਪੂਰਨ ਪਰਮੇਸੁਰਹ॥
Ant pooran parmaysureh

The Creator Lord has always existed.
That Infinite One existed in the beginning,
middle, and end;
unchanging, all pervading, and forever.

Union: To unite with the Infinite beyond time and space.

Aad is often defined as the beginning. Its meaning is actually more similar to "primal", or something that existed before the beginning, beyond and predating all that is. *Pooran* means complete; nothing else is needed to complete it. In the beginning, God was complete truth. *Madh pooran* means that in the middle God is completely whole, completely true, all-pervading. *Ant Pooran* means that in the end God will be the all-pervading *Parmaysureh*, the highest of high. The meaning is a lot like Guru Nanak Dev Ji's words at the beginning of Japji Sahib: *Aad Sach, Jugaad Sach, Hai Bhee Sach, Naanak Hosee Bhee Sach.*

Ang Sang Whaa-hay Guroo

Ang Sang is used throughout Gurbani.

ਅੰਗ ਸੰਗ ਵਾਹਿਗੁਰੂ
Ang Sang Whaa-hay Guroo

The Infinite Being is within me and vibrates in ecstasy in every molecule and cell of my being.

Ang is 'cell,' or 'limb.' *Sang* is 'in every part', or 'with every part'. *Whaa-hay* is the indescribable living ecstasy of Infinite Being. *Guroo* is wisdom or the knowledge that transforms your mind, emotions and essence.

Union: Synchronizes the finite sense of self to the Infinite Oneness.

Chanting this mantra, the dynamic, loving energy of the Infinite is dancing in every limb and every cell of our being. Individual consciousness merges with the Universal Consciousness. In this mantra, we experience that we are not alone. The Infinite One is with us in every cell and every limb of

our being. We feel the Divine Presence removing
our fears and loneliness. This mantra expresses
a universal truth. Repeating it creates a thought,
which gradually guides the psyche to adjust itself.
It reconnects every fragmented projection of
the psyche, each separated part of the body, and
synchronizes the finite to the Infinite. This act of
rejoining the separated parts is the quintessential
act of healing. Under attack, under war, under
the pressures of fear, this meditation keeps us
together, conscious, and ready to act. It brings
the inner peacefulness that comes only from the
touch and scope of spirit.

Too Kahay Doleh Praanee-aa

Guru Arjan Dev Ji
Raag Tilang
724

ਤੂ ਕਾਹੇ ਡੋਲਹਿ ਪ੍ਰਾਣੀਆ ਤੁਧੁ ਰਾਖੈਗਾ ਸਿਰਜਣਹਾਰੁ ॥
Too kaahay doleh praanee-aa tudh raakhaigaa sirjanhaar

Why do you waver, O mortal being?
The Creator Lord shall protect you.

Union: To overcome shortcomings and
achieve Divine Union.

Victory

Giaan Dhiaan Kichh Karam Na Jaanaa

Guru Arjan Dev Ji
Raag Soohee
750

ਗਿਆਨੁ ਧਿਆਨੁ ਕਿਛੁ ਕਰਮੁ ਨ ਜਾਣਾ ਸਾਰ ਨ ਜਾਣਾ ਤੇਰੀ॥
Giaan dhiaan kichh karam na jaanaa saar na jaanaa tayree.

ਸਭ ਤੇ ਵਡਾ ਸਤਿਗੁਰੁ ਨਾਨਕੁ ਜਿਨਿ ਕਲ ਰਾਖੀ ਮੇਰੀ॥
Sabh tay vadaa Satgur Naanak, jin kal raakhee mayree.

I do not know about wisdom, meditation, and good deeds.

I do not know about Your excellence.

Satguru is the greatest of all. My honor is saved.

Victory: Brings victory through selfless service.

Paataalaa Paataal Lakh

Guru Nanak Dev Ji
Japji Sahib
SGGS page 5

ਪਾਤਾਲਾ ਪਾਤਾਲ ਲਖ ਆਗਾਸਾ ਆਗਾਸ ॥
Paataalaa paataal lakh aagaasaa aagaas.

ਓੜਕ ਓੜਕ ਭਾਲਿ ਥਕੇ ਵੇਦ ਕਹਨਿ ਇਕ ਵਾਤ ॥
Orak orak bhaal thakay vayd kahan eik vaat.

ਸਹਸ ਅਠਾਰਹ ਕਹਨਿ ਕਤੇਬਾ ਅਸੁਲੂ ਇਕੁ ਧਾਤੁ ॥
Sahas athaareh kehan kataybaa asuloo eik dhaat.

ਲੇਖਾ ਹੋਇ ਤ ਲਿਖੀਐ ਲੇਖੈ ਹੋਇ ਵਿਣਾਸੁ ॥
Laykhaa ho-ei ta likhee-ai laykhai ho-ei vinaas.

ਨਾਨਕ ਵਡਾ ਆਖੀਐ ਆਪੇ ਜਾਣੈ ਆਪੁ ॥
Naanak vadaa aakhee-ai aapay jaanai aap.

There are nether worlds beneath nether worlds,

and hundreds of thousands of heavenly worlds above.

The Vedas say that you can search to find them all,
until you grow weary.

The scriptures say that there are 18,000 worlds,

but in reality there is only the one universe.

If you try to write an account of this,

your life will surely end before you finish writing it.

O Nanak, call Him great! He Himself knows Himself.

From the *Siri Guru Granth Sahib*, the 22nd pauree of Japji Sahib, Guru Nanak Dev Ji.

Victory: Gives you the strategy to bring victory in legal battles.

Santaa Kay Kaaraj Aap Khaloei-aa

Guru Arjan Dev Ji
Raag Soohee
783

ਸੰਤਾ ਕੇ ਕਾਰਜਿ ਆਪਿ ਖਲੋਇਆ ਹਰਿ ਕੰਮੁ ਕਰਾਵਣਿ ਆਇਆ ਰਾਮ॥
Santaa kay kaaraj aap khaloei-aa har kam karaavan aaei-aa raam.

The Lord has stood up to resolve the affairs of the Saints,
and has come to complete their tasks.

Victory: Brings victory and success in difficult situations.

Sat Siree Siree Akaal

This is traditionally attributed to Guru Gobind Singh Ji.

ਸਤਿ ਸ੍ਰੀ ਸ੍ਰੀ ਅਕਾਲ ਸ੍ਰੀ ਅਕਾਲ ਮਹਾਂ ਅਕਾਲ
Sat siree siree akaal, siree akaal mahaa(n) akaal

ਮਹਾਂ ਅਕਾਲ ਸਤਿਨਾਮ ਅਕਾਲ ਮੁਰਤ ਵਾਹਿਗੁਰੂ
Mahaa(n) akaal, satinaam, akaal moorat, Whaa-hay Guroo

The True Great, Great Deathless; Great Deathless beyond Death.
Beyond Death, Truth is His Name.
Deathless form of God, Experience of the Divine.

Victory: To give victory in all aspects of life.

This is called the mantra for the Aquarian Age. It helps overcome defeatist tendencies and gives courage and caliber. When we chant it we affirm that we are timeless, deathless beings. This is one of the "Aquarian Sadhana" mantras. When we are challenged in life there are three impulses we confront: To be alone or withdraw; to deny or fantasize about the future; or to live greedily or in scarcity. Chanting this mantra gives us the grit to keep up and be victorious and to live prosperously.

Thaapiaa Na Jaa-ei Keetaa Na Ho-ei

Guru Nanak Dev Ji
Japji Sahib
SGGS page 2

ਥਾਪਿਆ ਨ ਜਾਇ ਕੀਤਾ ਨ ਹੋਇ॥

Thaapiaa na jaa-ei, keetaa na ho-ei

ਆਪੇ ਆਪਿ ਨਿਰੰਜਨੁ ਸੋਇ॥

Aapay aap niranjan so-ei

ਜਿਨਿ ਸੇਵਿਆ ਤਿਨਿ ਪਾਇਆ ਮਾਨੁ॥

Jin sayviaa tin paaei-aa maan

ਨਾਨਕ ਗਾਵੀਐ ਗੁਣੀ ਨਿਧਾਨੁ॥

Naanak gaavee-ai gunee nidhaan

ਗਾਵੀਐ ਸੁਣੀਐ ਮਨਿ ਰਖੀਐ ਭਾਉ॥

Gaavee-ai sunee-ai man rakhee-ai bhaao

ਦੁਖੁ ਪਰਹਰਿ ਸੁਖੁ ਘਰਿ ਲੈ ਜਾਇ॥

Dukh parhar sukh ghar lai jaa-ei

ਗੁਰਮੁਖਿ ਨਾਦੰ ਗੁਰਮੁਖਿ ਵੇਦੰ ਗੁਰਮੁਖਿ ਰਹਿਆ ਸਮਾਈ ॥

Gurmukh naadang Gurmukh vaydang Gurmukh rehi-aa samaa-ee

ਗੁਰੁ ਈਸਰੁ ਗੁਰੁ ਗੋਰਖੁ ਬਰਮਾ ਗੁਰੁ ਪਾਰਬਤੀ ਮਾਈ ॥

Gur eesar Gur gorakh barmaa Gur paarbatee maa-ee

ਜੇ ਹਉ ਜਾਣਾ ਆਖਾ ਨਾਹੀ ਕਹਣਾ ਕਥਨੁ ਨ ਜਾਈ ॥

Jay hau jaanaa aakhaa naahee kehanaa kathan na jaa-ee

ਗੁਰਾ ਇਕ ਦੇਹਿ ਬੁਝਾਈ ॥

Guraa eik dayeh bujhaa-ee

ਸਭਨਾ ਜੀਆ ਕਾ ਇਕੁ ਦਾਤਾ ਸੋ ਮੈ ਵਿਸਰਿ ਨ ਜਾਈ ॥

Sabhanaa jee-aa kaa eik daataa so mai visar na jaa-ee

He cannot be established or created.

He Himself is immaculate and pure.

Those who serve Him are honored.

O Nanak, sing of the Lord, the treasure of virtue.

Sing and listen, and let your mind be filled with love.

Your troubles shall be taken far away,

And peace shall fill your heart and home.

The Guru's Word is the sound current of the Naad.

The Guru's Word is the wisdom of the Vedas.

The Guru's Word is pervading and permeating all.

The Guru is Shiva, the Guru is Vishnu and Brahma.

The Guru is Paarvati and Lakhshmi.

Even knowing God, I cannot describe Him.

He cannot be described in words.

The Guru has taught me one thing —

There is only One, the Giver of all souls.

May I never forget Him.

From the *Siri Guru Granth Sahib*, the 5th pauree of Japji Sahib, Guru Nanak Dev Ji.

Victory: Grants you all success.

The 5th pauree may be recited when you feel a sense of falure within yourself. When you feel that you are not up to the job, this pauree will grant total support.

Thir Ghar Baisaho

Guru Arjan Dev Ji
Raag Gauree
201

ਥਿਰੁ ਘਰਿ ਬੈਸਹੁ ਹਰਿ ਜਨ ਪਿਆਰੇ॥ ਸਤਿਗੁਰਿ ਤੁਮਰੇ ਕਾਜ ਸਵਾਰੇ॥

Thir ghar baisaho har jan piaaray, satgur tumray kaaj savaaray.

Remain steady in the home of your own self,
O beloved servant of the Lord.
The True Guru shall resolve all your affairs.

Victory: Brings victory over insurmountable odds.

Virtues

Jeea Jugat Vas Prabhoo Kai

Guru Arjan Dev Ji
Raag Bilaaval
818

ਜੀਅ ਜੁਗਤਿ ਵਸਿ ਪ੍ਰਭੁ ਕੈ ਜੋ ਕਹੈ ਸੁ ਕਰਨਾ॥
Jeea jugat vas prabhoo kai jo kahai so karnaa

The living creatures and their ways are in God's power.
Whatever God says, they do.

Virtues: To give you reverence and the grace of
your surroundings.

Saa Ray Gaa Maa Paa Dhaa Nee Saa Taa Naa Maa Raa Maa Dhaa Saa Saa Say So Hang – Khaoree Kriya

This mantra is attributed to Guru Arjan Dev ji.

ਸਾ ਰੇ ਗਾ ਮਾ ਪਾ ਧਾ ਨੀ ਸਾ ਤਾ ਨਾ ਮਾ ਰਾ ਮਾ ਧਾ ਸਾ ਸਾ ਸੇ ਸੋ ਹੰਗ

Saa Ray Gaa Maa Paa Dhaa Nee Saa Taa Naa Maa Raa Maa Dhaa Saa Saa Say So Hang

Virtues: Teaches you efficiency in self-sufficiency.

"Without self-sufficiency, there is deficiency and there is no efficiency. It is a very simple thing. Efficiency in self-sufficiency is minus deficiency."

– Yogi Bhajan

© The Teachings of Yogi Bhajan, October 8, 1987

The first seven sounds of this mantra represent a sargam, or musical scale. Each syllable is a note on the scale. Yogi Bhajan included this sargam when he taught this mantra and said that there are twenty sounds which can raise the consciousness from zero to infinity in the mortal. Saa Ray Gaa Maa Paa Dhaa Nee Saa Taa Naa Maa Raa Maa Dhaa Saa Saa Say So Hang. This is the totality. It is called Khaoree Kriya.

In these twenty sounds, when you breathe in one breath, and go through each note in tune, the entire harmony of the universe comes to you as a gift. There is nothing more harmonious. It is a creative tranquilizer and a peaceful objective sound current. Today, the "sound current" is being sold in the market, and many people will learn from it. Yet they may not know the basis of the sound current. The blessing of this mantra is that it gives you the basis of the sound current.

This mantra was given by Guru Arjan to the Sikhs, and Sikhs became musicians, poets, and very knowledgeable.

Sarab Nirantar Jee

Guru Raam Daas Ji
So Purakh
11

ਤੂੰ ਘਟ ਘਟ ਅੰਤਰਿ ਸਰਬ ਨਿਰੰਤਰਿ ਜੀ ਹਰਿ ਏਕੋ ਪੁਰਖੁ ਸਮਾਣਾ॥

Too(n) ghat ghat antar sarab nirantar jee har
ayko purkh samaanaa.

ਇਕਿ ਦਾਤੇ ਇਕਿ ਭੇਖਾਰੀ ਜੀ ਸਭਿ ਤੇਰੇ ਚੋਜ ਵਿਡਾਣਾ॥

Eik daatay eik bhaykhaaree jee sabh tayray choj vidhaanaa.

ਤੂੰ ਆਪੇ ਦਾਤਾ ਆਪੇ ਭੁਗਤਾ ਜੀ ਹਉ ਤੁਧੁ ਬਿਨੁ ਅਵਰੁ ਨ ਜਾਣਾ॥

Too(n) aapay daataa aapay bhugataa jee ho tudh bin avar na jaanaa.

ਤੂੰ ਪਾਰਬ੍ਰਹਮੁ ਬੇਅੰਤੁ ਬੇਅੰਤੁ ਜੀ ਤੇਰੇ ਕਿਆ ਗੁਣ ਆਖਿ ਵਖਾਣਾ॥

Too(n) paarbraham bayant bayant jee tayray kiaa gun aakh vakhaanaa.

ਜੋ ਸੇਵਹਿ ਜੋ ਸੇਵਹਿ ਤੁਧੁ ਜੀ ਜਨੁ ਨਾਨਕੁ ਤਿਨ ਕੁਰਬਾਣਾ॥

Jo sayveh jo sayveh tudh jee jan naanak tin kurbaanaa.

You are constant in each and every heart,
and in all things.

O Dear lord, You are the One.
Some are givers and some are beggars.

This is all Your wondrous play.
You Yourself are the giver,
and You Yourself are the enjoyer.

I know no other than You.

You are the supreme Lord God, limitless and infinite.
What virtues of Yours can I speak of and describe?
Unto those who serve You, unto those who serve You,
Dear Lord, servant Nanak is a sacrifice.

From the *Siri Guru Granth Sahib*, So Purkh, Guru Ram Das Ji.

Virtues: Grants you the virtues of humility and graceful manners.

This verse is part of So Purkh, the Sikh prayer recited during the twilight of the day.

Suni-ai Sidh Peer Sur Naath

Guru Nanak Dev Ji
Japji Sahib
SGGS page 2

ਸੁਣਿਐ ਸਿਧ ਪੀਰ ਸੁਰਿ ਨਾਥ॥
Suni-ai sidh peer sur naath

ਸੁਣਿਐ ਧਰਤਿ ਧਵਲ ਆਕਾਸ॥
Suni-ai dharat dhaval aakaas

ਸੁਣਿਐ ਦੀਪ ਲੋਅ ਪਾਤਾਲ॥
Suni-ai deep loa paataal

ਸੁਣਿਐ ਪੋਹਿ ਨ ਸਕੈ ਕਾਲੁ॥
Suni-ai poeh na sakai kaal

ਨਾਨਕ ਭਗਤਾ ਸਦਾ ਵਿਗਾਸੁ॥
Naanak bhagataa sadaa vigaas

ਸੁਣਿਐ ਦੂਖ ਪਾਪ ਕਾ ਨਾਸੁ॥
Suni-ai dookh paap kaa naas

ਸੁਣਿਐ ਈਸਰੁ ਬਰਮਾ ਇੰਦੁ॥
Suni-ai eesar barmaa eind

ਸੁਣਿਐ ਮੁਖਿ ਸਾਲਾਹਣ ਮੰਦੁ ॥

Suni-ai mukh saalaahan mand

ਸੁਣਿਐ ਜੋਗ ਜੁਗਤਿ ਤਨਿ ਭੇਦ ॥

Suni-ai jog jugat tan bhayd

ਸੁਣਿਐ ਸਾਸਤ ਸਿਮ੍ਰਿਤ ਵੇਦ ॥

Suni-ai saasat simrit vayd

ਨਾਨਕ ਭਗਤਾ ਸਦਾ ਵਿਗਾਸੁ ॥

Naanak bhagataa sadaa vigaas

ਸੁਣਿਐ ਦੂਖ ਪਾਪ ਕਾ ਨਾਸੁ ॥

Suni-ai dookh paap kaa naas

ਸੁਣਿਐ ਸਤੁ ਸੰਤੋਖੁ ਗਿਆਨੁ ॥

Suni-ai sat santokh giaan

ਸੁਣਿਐ ਅਠਸਠਿ ਕਾ ਇਸਨਾਨੁ ॥

Suni-ai athsath kaa eishnaan

ਸੁਣਿਐ ਪੜਿ ਪੜਿ ਪਾਵਹਿ ਮਾਨੁ ॥

Suni-ai par par paaveh maan

ਸੁਣਿਐ ਲਾਗੈ ਸਹਜਿ ਧਿਆਨੁ ॥

Suni-ai laagai sahej dhi-aan

ਨਾਨਕ ਭਗਤਾ ਸਦਾ ਵਿਗਾਸੁ ॥

Naanak bhagataa sadaa vigaas

ਸੁਨਿਐ ਦੂਖ ਪਾਪ ਕਾ ਨਾਸੁ ॥

Suni-ai dookh paap kaa naas

ਸੁਨਿਐ ਸਰਾ ਗੁਣਾ ਕੇ ਗਾਹ ॥

Suni-ai saraa gunaa kay gaah

ਸੁਨਿਐ ਸੇਖ ਪੀਰ ਪਾਤਿਸਾਹ ॥

Suni-ai shaykh peer paatishaah

ਸੁਨਿਐ ਅੰਧੇ ਪਾਵਹਿ ਰਾਹੁ ॥

Suni-ai andhay paaveh raaho

ਸੁਨਿਐ ਹਾਥ ਹੋਵੈ ਅਸਗਾਹੁ ॥

Suni-ai haath hovai asgaaho

ਨਾਨਕ ਭਗਤਾ ਸਦਾ ਵਿਗਾਸੁ ॥

Naanak bhagataa sadaa vigaas

ਸੁਨਿਐ ਦੂਖ ਪਾਪ ਕਾ ਨਾਸੁ ॥

Suni-ai dookh paap kaa naas

Listening to the Siddhas (beings of mastery),

the spiritual teachers, the heroic warriors,
the Yogic Masters;

listening to the earth, the ethers,
and the Akaashic Realms;

listening to the oceans, lands,
peoples of the world, and

the nether regions of the underworld;

listening, death cannot touch you.

O Nanak, the devotees are forever in bliss.

Listening, pain and sin are erased.

Listening one becomes as Shiva, Brahma, and Indra.

Listening, even foul-mouthed people praise Him.

Listening to the technologies of yoga,
and the secrets of the body;

listening to the Shaastras,
the Simritees, and the Vedas;

O Nanak, the devotees are forever in bliss.

Listening, pain and sin are erased.

Listening to truth, contentment,
and spiritual wisdom;

listening, as if to take one's cleansing bath

at the sixty-eight sacred shrines of pilgrimage;

listening and reciting, honor is obtained.

Listening intuitively, grasping the
essence of meditation,

O Nanak, the devotees are forever in bliss.

Listening, pain and sin are erased.

Listening, dive deep into the Ocean of Virtue.

Listening to Shaykhs (religious scholars),
spiritual teachers, and emperors;

listening, even the blind find their way.

Listening, the unreachable comes into our hands.

O Nanak, the devotees are forever in bliss.

Listening, pain and sin are erased.

Virtues: Instills the attributes of saintliness.

This mantra comes to us from the *Siri Guru Granth Sahib*, paurees 8–11 of Japji Sahib, by Guru Nanak. The 8th pauree of Japji Sahib gives the power to be a perfect sage. The 9th pauree gives expansion. The 10th pauree grants grace. The 11th pauree gives virtue. Recited all together the result is sainthood.

Wisdom

Aadays Tisai Aadays

Guru Nanak Dev Ji
Japji Sahib
SGGS page 6

ਆਦੇਸੁ ਤਿਸੈ ਆਦੇਸੁ ॥
Aadays tisai aadays

ਆਦਿ ਅਨੀਲੁ ਅਨਾਦਿ ਅਨਾਹਤਿ ਜੁਗੁ ਜੁਗੁ ਏਕੋ ਵੇਸੁ ॥
Aad aneel anaad anaahat jug jug ayko vays

I bow to You. I bow
again and again.

You are primal,
immaculate, eternal,
and immortal.
You are unchanging
through all the ages.

Wisdom: Instills knowledge of the Infinite.

This mantra is believed to instill the entire knowledge of the Universe without ever reading a book. It is the yogi's humble bowing to the Infinite.

"In this Slok, Guru Nanak Dev Ji totally completes the human anatomy, excellence, process, and projection in the most clear words that one can understand. He says it with absolute clarity, sparing nothing. Guru Nanak Dev Ji gives all salutations, Aadays, to God."

– Yogi Bhajan

© The Teachings of Yogi Bhajan, July 26, 1996

Asankh Naav Asankh Thaav

Guru Nanak Dev Ji
Japji Sahib
SGGS page 4

ਅਸੰਖ ਨਾਵ ਅਸੰਖ ਥਾਵ ॥
Asankh naav asankh thaav

ਅਗੰਮ ਅਗੰਮ ਅਸੰਖ ਲੋਅ ॥
Agamm agamm asankh loa

ਅਸੰਖ ਕਹਹਿ ਸਿਰਿ ਭਾਰੁ ਹੋਇ ॥
Asankh kaheh sir bhaar ho-ei

ਅਖਰੀ ਨਾਮੁ ਅਖਰੀ ਸਾਲਾਹ ॥
Akhree naam akhree saalaah

ਅਖਰੀ ਗਿਆਨੁ ਗੀਤ ਗੁਣ ਗਾਹ ॥
Akhree giaan geet gun gaah

ਅਖਰੀ ਲਿਖਣੁ ਬੋਲਣੁ ਬਾਣਿ ॥
Akhree likhan bolan baan

ਅਖਰਾ ਸਿਰਿ ਸੰਜੋਗੁ ਵਖਾਣਿ ॥
Akhraa sir sanjog vakhaan

ਜਿਨਿ ਏਹਿ ਲਿਖੇ ਤਿਸੁ ਸਿਰਿ ਨਾਹਿ॥

Jin ay-eh likhay tis sir naa-eh

ਜਿਵ ਫੁਰਮਾਏ ਤਿਵ ਤਿਵ ਪਾਹਿ॥

Jiv furmaa-ay tiv tiv paa-eh

ਜੇਤਾ ਕੀਤਾ ਤੇਤਾ ਨਾਉ॥

Jaytaa keetaa taytaa naa-o

ਵਿਣੁ ਨਾਵੈ ਨਾਹੀ ਕੋ ਥਾਉ॥

Vin naavai naahee ko thaa-o

ਕੁਦਰਤਿ ਕਵਣ ਕਹਾ ਵੀਚਾਰੁ॥

Kudrat kavan kahaa veechaar

ਵਾਰਿਆ ਨ ਜਾਵਾ ਏਕ ਵਾਰ॥

Vaariaa na jaavaa ayk vaar

ਜੋ ਤੁਧੁ ਭਾਵੈ ਸਾਈ ਭਲੀ ਕਾਰ॥

Jo tudh bhaavai saa-ee bhalee kaar

ਤੂ ਸਦਾ ਸਲਾਮਤਿ ਨਿਰੰਕਾਰ॥

Too sadaa salaamat nirankaar

Countless names, countless places;

unfathomable, inaccessible,
countless celestial realms —

even to call them countless is to carry the weight of
your mistakes on your head.

From the Word comes the Naam.
From the Word comes Your praises.

From the Word comes spiritual wisdom,
singing the songs of Your glory.

From the Word comes the written and
spoken words, and hymns.

From the Word comes one's destiny,
written upon the forehead.

But the One who wrote these words of destiny —

His forehead is not written upon.

As He ordains, so do we receive.

The created universe is the manifestation of Your Name.

Without Your Name, there is no place at all.

How can Your creative power be described?

I cannot even once be a sacrifice unto You.

Whatever pleases You is the only good done.

You the eternal and formless one.

Wisdom: Brings universal knowledge, inspiration, and revelation.

This mantra comes to us from the Siri Guru Granth Sahib, the 19th pauree of Japji, written by Guru Nanak. If you understand this pauree, you will never have trouble understanding anything.

Panch Parvaan Panch Pardhaan

Guru Nanak Dev Ji
Japji Sahib
SGGS Page 3

ਪੰਚ ਪਰਵਾਣ ਪੰਚ ਪਰਧਾਨੁ ॥
Panch parvaan panch pardhaan

ਪੰਚੇ ਪਾਵਹਿ ਦਰਗਹਿ ਮਾਨੁ ॥
Panchay paaveh dargeh maan

ਪੰਚੇ ਸੋਹਹਿ ਦਰਿ ਰਾਜਾਨੁ ॥
Panchay soheh dar raajaan

ਪੰਚਾ ਕਾ ਗੁਰੁ ਏਕੁ ਧਿਆਨੁ ॥
Panchaa kaa gur ayk dhi-aan

ਜੇ ਕੋ ਕਹੈ ਕਰੈ ਵੀਚਾਰੁ ॥
Jay ko kehai karai veechaar

ਕਰਤੇ ਕੈ ਕਰਣੈ ਨਾਹੀ ਸੁਮਾਰੁ ॥
Kartay kai karnai naahee sumaar

ਧੌਲੁ ਧਰਮੁ ਦਇਆ ਕਾ ਪੂਤੁ ॥
Dhaol dharam dei-aa kaa poot

ਸੰਤੋਖੁ ਥਾਪਿ ਰਖਿਆ ਜਿਨਿ ਸੂਤਿ॥

Santokh thaap rakhi-aa jin soot

ਜੇ ਕੋ ਬੁਝੈ ਹੋਵੈ ਸਚਿਆਰੁ॥

Jay ko bujhai hovai sachi-aar

ਧਵਲੈ ਉਪਰਿ ਕੇਤਾ ਭਾਰੁ॥

Dhavalai upar kaytaa bhaar

ਧਰਤੀ ਹੋਰੁ ਪਰੈ ਹੋਰੁ ਹੋਰੁ॥

Dhartee hor parai hor hor

ਤਿਸ ਤੇ ਭਾਰੁ ਤਲੈ ਕਵਣੁ ਜੋਰੁ॥

Tis tay bhaar talai kavan jor

ਜੀਅ ਜਾਤਿ ਰੰਗਾ ਕੇ ਨਾਵ॥

Jee-a jaat rangaa kay naav

ਸਭਨਾ ਲਿਖਿਆ ਵੁੜੀ ਕਲਾਮ॥

Sabhanaa likhi-aa vuree kalaam

ਏਹੁ ਲੇਖਾ ਲਿਖਿ ਜਾਣੈ ਕੋਇ॥

Ayho laykhaa likh jaanai ko-ei

ਲੇਖਾ ਲਿਖਿਆ ਕੇਤਾ ਹੋਇ॥

Laykhaa likhi-aa kaytaa ho-ei

ਕੇਤਾ ਤਾਣੁ ਸੁਆਲਿਹੁ ਰੂਪੁ॥

Kaytaa taan su-aaliho roop

ਕੇਤੀ ਦਾਤਿ ਜਾਣੈ ਕੌਣੁ ਕੂਤੁ॥

Kaytee daat jaanai kaon koot

ਕੀਤਾ ਪਸਾਉ ਏਕੋ ਕਵਾਉ॥

Keetaa pasaa-o ayko kavaa-o

ਤਿਸ ਤੇ ਹੋਏ ਲਖ ਦਰੀਆਉ॥

Tis tay ho-ay lakh daree-aa-o

ਕੁਦਰਤਿ ਕਵਣ ਕਹਾ ਵੀਚਾਰੁ॥

Kudrat kavan kahaa veechaar

ਵਾਰਿਆ ਨ ਜਾਵਾ ਏਕ ਵਾਰ॥

Vaari-aa na jaavaa ayk vaar

ਜੋ ਤੁਧੁ ਭਾਵੈ ਸਾਈ ਭਲੀ ਕਾਰ॥

Jo tudh bhaavai saa-ee bhalee kaar

ਤੂ ਸਦਾ ਸਲਾਮਤਿ ਨਿਰੰਕਾਰ॥

Too sadaa salaamat nirankaar

The Chosen Ones, the self-elect,
are accepted and honored.

The Chosen Ones are honored
in the court of the Lord.

The Chosen Ones look beautiful
in the courts of kings.

The Chosen Ones meditate single-mindedly
upon the Guru.

No matter how much anyone tries to
explain and describe them,

The doings of the Creator cannot be listed.

The mythical bull is Dharma,
the son of compassion.

This is what patiently holds the earth in its place.

One who understands this becomes truthful.

What a great load this puts on the bull!

So many worlds beyond this world —
so very many!

What power holds them
and supports their weight?

The names and colors of the various species of beings

were all written by the everflowing pen of God.

Who knows how to write this account?

Imagine what a huge scroll it would be!

What power! What fascinating beauty!

And what gifts! Who can know them all?

With one sound, You created the
expanse of the universe.

Hundreds of thousands of rivers began to flow.

How can Your creative power be described?

I cannot even once be a sacrifice unto You.

Whatever pleases You is the only good done,

O Thou, eternal and formless One.

Wisdom: Gives knowledge of the structure of
the universe.

This mantra comes to us from the Siri Guru
Granth Sahib, the 16th pauree of Japji Sahib, by
Guru Nanak. Reciting this pauree will heighten
your perception of the Divine in all things. It will
help you to know the power of compassion and its
potential to elevate.

Tayree Meher Daa Bolnaa

ਤੇਰੀ ਮਿਹਰ ਦਾ ਬੋਲਣਾ
Tayree meher daa bolnaa

ਤੁਧੁ ਆਗੈ ਅਰਦਾਸ
Tudh aagai ardaas

ਗੁਰੂ ਗੁਰੂ ਵਾਹਿਗੁਰੂ
Guroo Guroo Whaa-hay Guroo

ਗੁਰੂ ਰਾਮਦਾਸ
Guroo Raam Daas

ਆਦਿ ਗੁਰਏ ਨਮਹ॥
Aad Guray nameh

ਜੁਗਾਦਿ ਗੁਰਏ ਨਮਹ॥
Jugaad Guray nameh

ਸਤਿਗੁਰਏ ਨਮਹ॥
Sat Guray nameh

ਸ੍ਰੀ ਗੁਰਦੇਵਏ ਨਮਹ॥
Siree Gurdayv ay nameh

Oh Guru Ram Das, this is my prayer to You.

May my words be from You and may my mind be a source of knowledge and ecstasy.

May Wisdom come as I act as a servant of the Infinite.

I bow to the Primal Guru.

I bow to the Guru throughout the ages.

I bow to the Guru that is true here and now.

I bow to the Great Guru that will always and forever be.

Wisdom: To seek the highest wisdom to prevail always in our lives, to bring in healing miracles, and to cover our mistakes.

This mantra calls on the wisdom of the ages, the great Divine and transparent Guru, the True Guru. This is the mantra that Yogi Bhajan chanted before he lectured. He tuned in to Guru Ram Das, and the Golden Chain of Teachers that have passed wisdom down on this planet for millennia. If you let the consciousness of Guru Ram Das into your heart, it is between you and Him as to what happens. There will be no doubt; there will be healing and grace.

Whaa-hay Guroo

ਵਾਹਿਗੁਰੂ
Whaa-hay Guroo

No literal English translation. Whaa-hay is indescribable bliss and *Guroo* brings us from darkness to light. *Whaa-hay Guroo* is complete ecstasy in Divine Wisdom.

Wisdom: Brings the wisdom of the Infinite and Divine ecstasy.

This mantra expresses the indescribable ecstasy of the experience of going from darkness to light, from ignorance to true understanding. It is the Infinite Teacher of the soul. A *Trikutee* mantra, it balances the energies of the generating, organizing, and transforming principles. Yogi Bhajan taught that G-O-D is the Generator, Organizer, and Destroyer (in the sense of transformative destruction). It expresses ecstasy through knowledge and experience. It is the Gurmantra, which triggers the destiny. It is said that chanting *Whaa-hay Guroo* once is equivalent to chanting *Har* 11,000 times.

Whaa-hay Guroo Whaa-hay Guroo Whaa-hay Guroo Whaa-hay Jeeo

Bhatt Gayandh
Svaiyay Mehl 5
page 1402

ਵਾਹਿਗੁਰੂ ਵਾਹਿਗੁਰੂ ਵਾਹਿਗੁਰੂ ਵਾਹਿ ਜੀਓ ॥

Whaa-hay Guroo Whaa-hay Guroo Whaa-hay Guroo Whaa-hay Jeeo

Whaa-hay *Guroo* – Great Beyond description is the experience of God's Wisdom.

Jeeo – The experience of the soul merged in the Divine

Wisdom: Brings indescribable wisdom and the ecstasy of dwelling in God.

This is the mantra of Infinity that takes us from darkness to light, from ignorance to true understanding. It awakens the sixth center of consciousness, the pituitary gland or the third eye. It is the Divine Teacher of the soul. It is the Guru mantra, which triggers the destiny and expresses ecstasy through knowledge and experience. *Wahe Guru* gives the experience of the Divine and also imparts an affectionate relationship with the Divine. Yogi Bhajan said that this mantra gives us a clear perception of what is important to preserve and that it links the essence of our purpose to the greater minds and souls in the Cosmos. This is one of the Aquarian Sadhana mantras.

Mantras & Prayers from Various Spiritual Traditions

Some of the mantras and prayers in this section are in English and are taught frequently in the practice of Kundalini Yoga. During his time in the West, the Siri Singh Sahib taught some of these mantras and in other cases adopted prayers that have existed in various spiritual traditions. He always told us that the power of the Word comes through in the frequency of the prayer and projection of the sound current, in any language.

Eik Ong Kaar Sat Naam Siree Whaa-hay Guroo Adi Shakti Mantra

ਇਕ ਓਅੰਕਾਰ ਸਤਿਨਾਮ ਸਿਰੀ ਵਾਹਿਗੁਰੂ ॥
Eik Ong Kaar Sat Naam Siree Whaa-hay Guroo

The Creator and the Creation are One.
This is our True Identity.
The ecstasy of the experience of this wisdom is
beyond all words and brings indescribable bliss.

This is inscribed on the wall of the Baoli Sahib (the Well with 84
steps) at the Goindwal Sahib Gurdwara in India.

Mastery: Brings kundalini awakening, opening of
the chakras and an experience of bliss.

This mantra takes our consciousness from
individual consciousness, to group consciousness,
to Universal Consciousness. Also called Long Ek
Ong Kar or Morning Call, this was the first mantra
taught by Yogi Bhajan in the U.S. in its long form.

How to chant this mantra in the long form:
Yogi Bhajan gave a 2 ½ breath cycle to chant this
mantra in the long form. Inhale deeply through the
nose and chant *"Eik Ong Kaar"*.

Eik is chanted quickly, *Ong* is held until the breath is halfway through, and *Kaar* is held for the remaining half of the breath. Inhale deeply through the nose a second time and chant *"Sat Naam, Siree"*. *Sat* is chanted quickly and then *Naam* is chanted and held for nearly the entire length of the breath. At the very end of the second breath chant *Siree*. Then take a half breath and chant *"Whaa-hay Guroo"*. This completes one 2 ½ breath cycle.

Yogi Bhajan called this the *Mantra of the Aquarian Age* and said it would enable us to raise our frequency to match the planetary transition in the new age. This mantra is chanted in its long form every morning at the beginning of the Aquarian Sadhana (as given in 1992), and it is the only mantra that has been included in every sadhana given by Yogi Bhajan since he started teaching in America. The original sadhana he gave was to chant this mantra in its long form for 2 ½ hours before the rising of the sun.

This mantra is also chanted and sung in many different melodies and rhythms.

Alakh Baabaa Siree Chand Dee Rakh

ਅਲੱਖ ਬਾਬਾ ਸਿਰੀ ਚੰਦ ਦੀ ਰਖ॥
Alakh Baabaa Siree Chand Dee Rakh

Hail Baba Siri Chand, the Protector against unseen attacks.

Protection: Protects one from a psychic attack.

This mantra calls upon the help of Baba Siri Chand, who was the elder son of Guru Nanak Dev Ji, the first Sikh Guru. If one is under an unseen or a psychic attack, this mantra will reflect the energy back. Yogi Bhajan taught that this mantra is only to be chanted once per day.

Dhartee Hai Aakaash Hai

ਧਰਤੀ ਹੈ ਆਕਾਸ਼ ਹੈ ਗੁਰੂ ਰਾਮਦਾਸ ਹੈ॥
Dhartee Hai Aakaash Hai Guroo Raam Daas Hai

The Earth is. The Ethers are. Guru Ram Das is.

Prosperity: Attracts opportunities for prosperity.

This mantra makes you present. Additionally, this mantra keeps you humble and effective on your new ventures. Practice this mantra with visualization of the self within the cosmos, to connect the earth and the vastness of the ethers. Project the mantra from your heart and call on your highest spirit.

Gobinday Gobinday Haree Haree

ਗੋਬਿੰਦੇ ਗੋਬਿੰਦੇ ਹਰੀ ਹਰੀ॥
Gobinday Gobinday Haree Haree

God, the Sustainer and Support of All

God, the creative energy that inherently
exists within each of us —
fresh, beautiful, potent healing

Self-esteem: Uplifts your spirit and builds
your self-confidence.

God and Me, Me and God, are One

God and Me, Me and God, are One

Self-esteem: Connects you directly to your own Divine consciousness and builds your confidence, grace, and self-image.

This is an affirmation mantra given by Yogi Bhajan to remember that God is within everyone, and that to connect to the Divine you need only to look within.

Guroo Guroo Whaa-hay Guroo

ਗੁਰੂ ਗੁਰੂ ਵਾਹਿਗੁਰੂ ਗੁਰੂ ਰਾਮਦਾਸ ਗੁਰ
Guroo Guroo Whaa-hay Guroo, Guroo Raam Daas Guroo

Great is the wisdom that flows
through the one who serves the Infinite.

Guroo – teacher or guide that brings one from darkness to light.

Whaa-hay – exclamation of ecstasy like "WOW!"

Raam Daas – literally translates as "God's Servant", but also refers to the consciousness of Guru Ram Das, the Fourth Guru of the Sikhs.

Miracles: To bring miracles into your life.

This mantra gathers the healing and protective energy of Guru Ram Das. Yogi Bhajan taught that even if you are at the end of your rope and everything has been tried and failed, you can chant this mantra and expect a miracle. He gave a specific yogic technique for chanting this mantra, as follows:

Inhale deeply and chant *Guroo Guroo Whaa-hay Guroo, Guroo Raam Daas Guroo* five times on one breath. Each of the five repetitions changes the impact of the sound and its projection and creates a balance of the five elements. This mantra was given to Yogi Bhajan by Guru Ram Das in His astral self-projection. It relates directly to healing and protective energy represented by Guru Ram Das. As the fourth Guru of the Sikhs, Guru Ram Das was known for humility and healing. This mantra is also known for its healing qualities and for imparting humility to the one who chants it. The mantra is comprised of two parts. The first part is a Nirgun (Infinite) mantra (Guru Guru Wahe Guru). This projects the mind to the source of knowledge and ecstasy. The second part is a Sirgun (finite) mantra (Guru Ram Das Guru). This embodies the wisdom that flows through a servant of the Infinite. It is the mantra of humility which brings the experience of the finite to Infinity.

Har Haray Haree

ਹਰਿ ਹਰੇ ਹਰੀ ॥
Har haray haree

The three phases of *"Har"*, Divine Creation:

Har	Seed
Haray	Flow
Haree	Completion

Prosperity: Produces vitality and prosperity.

Invoking creative manifestation of *Har*, this mantra projects the primal force of creation to complete prosperity.

Haree Naam Sat Naam

ਹਰੀ ਨਾਮ ਸਤਿ ਨਾਮ ਹਰੀ ਨਾਮ ਹਰੀ॥
Haree naam sat naam haree naam haree

ਹਰੀ ਨਾਮ ਸਤਿ ਨਾਮ ਸਤਿ ਨਾਮ ਹਰੀ॥
Haree naam sat naam sat naam haree

Haree – Creative flow of life
Naam – Identity
Sat – Truth

Prosperity: Brings abundance in health and wealth.

This is a prosperity mantra that uplifts you. The first part of this mantra aligns the creative flow of life (Hari) with your personal identity (Naam) to bring you to your highest destiny. The second part aligns your creative intuition and your identified intention with the unseen hand of Truth in spirit and supports the fulfillment of your highest potential.

Hargobind Hargobind Hargobind Mahaan Hai

ਹਰਿਗੋਬਿੰਦ ਹਰਿਗੋਬਿੰਦ ਹਰਿਗੋਬਿੰਦ ਮਹਾਨ ਹੈ॥
Hargobind Hargobind Hargobind Mahaan Hai

ਸਰਬ ਸ਼ਕਤੀ ਸਰਬ ਸ਼ਕਤੀ ਸਰਬ ਸ਼ਕਤੀ ਮਹਾਨ ਹੈ।
Sarab Shaktee Sarab Shaktee Sarab Shaktee Mahaan Hai

Great is *Hargobind*, sustainer of the world.

Great is *Sarab Shakti*, Divine power in all forms.

Protection: Divine protection for property, health, and wealth.

This is a powerful sound current to ward off sickness and misfortune and call on Divine protection for yourself and your family.

Healthy Am I, Happy Am I, Holy Am I

Healthy am I, Happy am I, Holy am I

Elevation: Brings personal blessings and upliftment.

This mantra is the blessing affirmation of Yogi Bhajan's firm belief that everyone has the right to live *healthy, happy, and holy*.

Hamee Ham Brahm Ham

ਹਮੀ ਹਮ ਬ੍ਰਹਮ ਹਮ॥
Hamee Ham Brahm Ham

We are we in Spirit. We are God. This mantra literally means that we are the spirit of God. It is total spirit. Total spirit represents the Divine Master and it fixes the identity in its true reality.

Trust: Eliminates the ego consciousness of separation and loss and builds faith and trust in the Infinite.

Hamee Ham Tumee Tum Whaa-hay Guroo

ਹਮੀ ਹਮ ਤੁਮੀ ਤੁਮ ਵਾਹਿਗੁਰ
Hamee Ham Tumee Tum Whaa-hay Guroo

I am Thine in Mine Myself, Whaa-hay Guru

Destiny: Brings a sense of personal purpose and discovery of your highest destiny.

This mantra brings a profound connectedness with other people and opens the heart and mind to recognize God in all that is. It was given as the First Sutra of the Aquarian Age: *Recognize the Other Person Is You.* It has a subtle structure in its sound, beat, and arrangement. We vibrate it from within our heart and listen to our sound and become merged in it. It stimulates realization of oneself as one with the Divine. In this way our mind easily accepts the premise of the First Sutra, *Recognize the Other Person Is You*, beyond all our conscious and subconscious resistances. All that is inside and all that is outside come together and are expanded in *Wahe Guru*. The heart center and throat center are engaged. On the sound of *hay*, the flow of power and energy is felt gently at the brow center to complete the projection.

I Am Bountiful, Blissful, and Beautiful

I Am Bountiful, Blissful, and Beautiful.
Bountiful, Blissful, and Beautiful I am.

Trust: Affirms trust in the Infinite and builds
self-confidence and self-esteem as we learn to
love ourselves.

I Am Happy, I Am Good

I Am Happy, I Am Good

I Am Happy, I Am Good

Sat Naam Sat Naam Sat Naam Jee

Whaa-hay Guroo Whaa-hay Guroo Whaa-hay Guroo Jee

Self-esteem: A blessing for children, to inspire confidence, self-worth and self-love.

This is an affirmation given by Yogi Bhajan specifically for children to sing and grow into their own dignity, divinity, and grace. It's a great way to instill an understanding of the power of words, mantras and affirmations, and it gives children an inspiring boost to their confidence and self-esteem.

I Am the Light of My Soul

I am the light of my soul.

I am beautiful, I am bountiful, I am bliss.

I am, I am.

Love: To infuse love of the Divine self.

This mantra is an affirmation given by Yogi Bhajan to fill the gaps in our upbringing with love of the Divine self and to learn to honor that true reality in all beings.

© The Teachings of Yogi Bhajan, July 7, 1994

I Am, I Am

I Am, I Am

Self-Realization: Connects the finite and Infinite identities.

The first *"I Am"* emphasizes "I" as the personal, finite sense of self. The second *"I Am"* emphasizes "Am" as the impersonal and transcendent sense of Self. All real mantras blend this polarity of the finite and Infinite in their internal structure and design. If you only say the first *"I Am"* the mind will automatically try to answer, "I am what?" That question sends the mind on a search through all the categories and roles that hold the finite identities. If you immediately say the second part of the mantra, *"I Am"*, the thought becomes " I Am What I Am". To be what you are is the essence of Truth and will lead you to the nature of True Reality.

Jo Guroo Raam Daas Ko Dhiaa-ay

Source: Furmaan Khalsa page 214
Author: Sir Singh Sahib Bhai Sahib Bhai Sahib Harbhajan Singh Khalsa Yogiji

ਰਾਮ ਕ੍ਰਿਸ਼ਨਾ ਬੁਧ ਕਾ ਨਾਮ॥
Raam Krishnaa Budh kaa naam

ਮੂਸਾ ਈਸਾ ਮੁਹੰਮਦ ਕਾ ਕਲਾਮ॥
Moosaa Eesaa Muhammad kaa kalaam

ਪੂਜਾ ਆਰਤੀ ਨਮਾਜ ਸਲਾਮ॥
Poojaa aartee namaaj salaam

ਚਰਨ ਪਾਹੁਲ ਅੰਮ੍ਰਿਤ ਕਾ ਜਾਮ॥
Charan paahul amrit kaa jaam

ਰਾਜ ਜੋਗ ਬ੍ਰਹਮ ਕਾ ਧਾਮ॥
Raaj jog brahm kaa dhaam

ਜੋਗ ਧਿਆਨ ਹਰੀ ਕਾ ਨਾਮ॥
Yog dhiaan haree kaa naam

ਇਨ ਸਭ ਕੋ ਅੰਤਰ ਮੇ ਪਾਏ॥
Ein sabh ko antar may paa-ay

ਜੋ ਗੁਰੂ ਰਾਮ ਦਾਸ ਕੋ ਧਿਆਏ॥
Jo Guroo Raam Daas ko dhiaa-ay

ਰਾਜ ਕਾਜ ਬ੍ਰਹਮ ਕਾ ਯੋਗ॥
Raaj kaaj brahm kaa yog

ਸਵਰਨ ਸੁੰਦਰੀ ਪਦਾਰਥ ਭੋਗ॥
Savaran sundree padaarath bhog

ਬ੍ਰਹਮਾ ਵਿਸ਼ਨੂੰ ਅਤੇ ਮਹੇਸ਼॥
Brahmaa Vishnoo atay Mahaysh

ਨਰਾਇਣ ਹਰੀ ਬ੍ਰਹਮ ਉਪਦੇਸ਼॥
Naraa-ein haree brahm updaysh

ਰਿਧਿ ਸਿਧ ਅਉਰ ਨੌ ਨਿਧਿ॥
Ridh sidh aaur nau nidh

ਲਾਲ ਜਵਾਹਰ ਮਾਇਆ ਕੀ ਬਿਧ॥
Laal javaahar maaei-aa kee bidh

ਇਨ ਸਭ ਕੋ ਅੰਤਰ ਮੇ ਪਾਏ॥
Ein sabh ko antar may paa-ay

ਜੋ ਗੁਰੂ ਰਾਮ ਦਾਸ ਕੋ ਧਿਆਏ॥
Jo Guroo Raam Daas ko dhiaa-ay

The Names of Rama,
Krishna, and Buddha,

The words of Moses,
Jesus, and Muhammad,

Devotions, Salutations,
Praises, and Prayers,

The wash of the Saint's feet,
the cup of Nectar,

The realm of Raj Yoga,
the Lord's own mansion,

God's Name and Yoga and
Concentration,

All of these shall be granted unto

Those who meditate on
Ram Das the Guru.

The Royal Marriage,
Union with Brahm,

Gold and beauty and
worldly pleasures,

Brahma, Vishnu,
and Lord Mahesh,

The teachings of Hari,
Narayan, and Brahm,

Earthly wealth, magic powers, and
all the nine treasures,

Rubies and diamonds and
all Maya's pleasures,

All of these shall be granted unto

Those who meditate on
Ram Das the Guru.

From the Furmaan Khalsa, Siri Singh Sahib Bhai Sahib
Harbhajan Singh Khalsa Yogiji (Yogi Bhajan)

Enlightenment: To live successfully with an open
heart and mind, and with an experience of your
infinity.

Laya Yoga Mantra

ਇਕ ਓਅੰਕਾਰ ॥
Eik Ong Kaar(uh)

ਸਾ ਤਾ ਨਾ ਮਾ
Saa Taa Naa Maa(uh)

ਸ੍ਰੀ ਵਾਹਿਗੁਰੂ ॥
Siree Whaa(uh), hay Guroo

There is one Creator of all Creation.
True is the Name and great is the blessing of the One Lord.

Self-Realization: Gives you consciousness of your soul and your destiny in the present moment.

This extraordinary Laya Yoga chant refers to suspension from the ordinary world. Laya Yoga fixes your attention and energy on your essence and higher consciousness without normal distractions and attachments having power over your reactive awareness. The practice of Laya Yoga chanting suspends you above any conflicts due to attractions of success and the activity of the Positive Mind. This allows your activity to serve your purpose. It makes you creative and focused on your real priorities and helps you sacrifice what is needed to accomplish them.

This mantra opens the secret book of Laya Yoga. It enables you to remember and experience consciously the link between you and the Creator. Practice the mantra for 40–120 days. It will etch into the subconscious the memory and experience of your true identity.

This mantra was guarded like a secret gem. It is the key to the inner doors of Naad, the realm of creative sound. If you listen to the sound of the mantra and then concentrate on its subtle sounds, you will become absorbed into the unlimited domain of your higher self. The mantra has a structure of 3 ½ cycles in its spin. Each "Uh" sound lifts the diaphragm, which commutes the energy of prana and apana across the heart area. That transformation is one cycle. The cycle of 3 ½ is the pulse rhythm of the kundalini itself. This is why the kundalini is often represented as coiled 3 ½ times. As with all other genuine mantras, it is discovered by the seer who travels in the subtle realms of consciousness. It has been confirmed by countless practitioners who adopted the discipline of this meditation. The inner sounds can be heard at different levels of subtlety.

Maa

ਮਾਂ

Maa

Universal Divine Mother

Divine Mother: Merge into the Divine essence of the Universal Mother.

This mantra is repeated over and over to connect with the essence of the Universal Mother. In the Himalayas there was a yogi who knew this meditation. Yogi Bhajan tracked him for three months, and then waited in Gurupranam (a yoga posture) outside his home for two days to get it.

On This Day

On this day the Lord gave you life —

May you use it to serve Him.

All of our loving prayers will be with you —

May you never forget Him.

May the long time sun shine upon you,

All love surround you,

And the pure light within you

Guide your way on.

Sat Naam.

Ecstasy: A divine birthday blessing.

This is the 3HO birthday blessing song. The first part was written by MSS[1] Livtar Singh Khalsa, and the second part is the 3HO[2] prayer sung at the end of every yoga class.

---

1   Mukhia Singh Sahib (MSS): Ministerial title from Sikh Dharma International given to a man who has performed exceptional service to the community. www.sikhdharma.org/pages/glossary

2   3HO (Healthy, Happy, Holy Organization) promotes a lifestyle that supports "householders" (ordinary workers and family people) as they pursue transformation of consciousness. www.3HO.org

Ong Kaar Nirankaar
Nirankaar Ong

ਓਅੰਕਾਰ ਨਿਰੰਕਾਰ
Ong kaar nirankaar

ਨਿਰੰਕਾਰ ਓਅੰ ॥
Nirankaar ong

The form of the creation and the formless Creator

Union: Brings union from separation.

Ong Namo Guroo Dayv Namo – Adi Mantra

ੴ ਨਮੋ ਗੁਰੂ ਦੇਵ ਨਮੋ ॥
Ong Namo Guroo Dayv Namo

I bow to the One Infinite Creative Wisdom,
I bow to the Divine teacher within.

Enlightenment: Tunes us into our highest Divine wisdom.

Ong Namo Guru Dev Namo, also known as the Adi Mantra, is chanted before teaching a Kundalini Yoga class, to bring us into our highest Divine wisdom, invoking the consciousness of the golden chain of the teachers of Raaj Yoga. It may be chanted at any time to invoke one's most Divine meditative state.

Ong Namo Guroo Dayv Namo Guroo Dayv Namo Guroo Dayvaa

ੴ ਨਮੋ ਗੁਰੂ ਦੇਵ ਨਮੋ, ਗੁਰੂ ਦੇਵ ਨਮੋ ਗੁਰੂ ਦੇਵਾ

Ong Namo Guroo Dayv Namo Guroo Dayv Namo Guroo Dayvaa

I bow to the Universal Creative Wisdom,
I bow to the Divine Teacher.

Enlightenment: Tunes us into the total spiritual knowledge of all teachers who have ever existed or who will ever exist on this Earth.

This is the Complete Adi Mantra. If you are teaching in any other capacity other than Kundalini and wish to tune into your higher consciousness, chant this mantra silently in its complete form before you begin. You may also use the complete form anytime you experience a lack of faith. Many of you will enter Shakti Pad, or you are in it, and this mantra will help.

"When this mantra is chanted five times on one breath, the total spiritual knowledge of all teachers who have ever existed or who will ever exist on this Earth, is located in that person."

– Yogi Bhajan

© The Teachings of Yogi Bhajan, August 22, 1978

Ong Sohang

ੴ ਸੋਹੰ

Ong Sohang

Ong – The Creative Consciousness of the Universe

Sohang – I am that!

Intuition: Awakens creative intuition and stimulates opening the heart chakra and knowing oneness with all that is.

Chanting this mantra brings inner realization and recognition that each of us is a part of the Creative Consciousness of the Universe.

Raa Raa Raa Raa Maa Maa Maa Maa Raamaa Raamaa Raamaa Raam Saa Taa Naa Maa

ਰਾ ਰਾ ਰਾ ਰਾ
Raa Raa Raa Raa

ਮਾ ਮਾ ਮਾ ਮਾ
Maa Maa Maa Maa

ਰਾਮਾ ਰਾਮਾ ਰਾਮਾ ਰਾਮ
Raamaa Raamaa Raamaa Raam

ਸਾ ਤਾ ਨਾ ਮਾ
Saa Taa Naa Maa

Ra represents the sun or masculine energy.
Ma represents the moon or feminine energy.
Sa Ta Na Ma represents the cycle of life:

Communication: Opens the neutral mind and clears communication blocks.

Raa Raa Raa Raa Maa Maa Maa Maa Saa Saa Saa Sat Haree Har Haree Har

ਰਾ ਰਾ ਰਾ ਰਾ

Raa Raa Raa Raa

ਮਾ ਮਾ ਮਾ ਮਾ

Maa Maa Maa Maa

ਸਾ ਸਾ ਸਾ ਸਤਿ

Saa Saa Saa Sat

ਹਰੀ ਹਰਿ ਹਰੀ ਹਰਿ

Haree Har Haree Har

Ra – Sun Energy, Masculine, Positive, Generating Force.

Ma – Moon Energy, Feminine, Receptive Force.

Sa/Sat – Impersonal Infinity, Truth.

Hari/Har – Creative Infinity.

Healing: Balances the masculine and feminine energies of the body, the hemispheres of the brain and the sense of identity.

Raam Raam Haree Raam

ਰਾਮ ਰਾਮ ਹਰੀ ਰਾਮ, ਰਾਮ ਰਾਮ ਹਰੀ ਹਰੀ
Raam Raam Haree Raam, Raam Raam Haree Haree

Raa is sun. Maa is moon.
Together, they are Raam,
God's creativity.
Haree is the seed of God in the
manifestation of the creation.

Self-Realization: To take you beyond polarity to experience and project your original self.

This is a special Naad that preceded the Panj Shabad, Sa Ta Na Ma. Yogi Bhajan taught that it has a distinct structure to each movement of the sound. The first *Ram* invokes the creativity and blessing of the universal magnetic field and existence. The second *Ram* consolidates and protects that magnetic field and creation. The third *Ram* completes and gives peace through the time of death. *Hari,* as the final two words, is the platform of the four corners that elevates you in consciousness as you journey across earth. The first half of the mantra is a relationship in Naad to the Infinite and formless existence and non-existence. The second half is guidance through the experiences of form and earth. Together the two parts of this mantra are a polarity that takes you beyond polarity to experience and project your original self.

Saa Taa Naa Maa Raa Maa Daa Saa Saa Say So Hang

ਸਾ ਤਾ ਨਾ ਮਾ ਰਾ ਮਾ ਦਾ ਸਾ ਸਾ ਸੇ ਸੋ ਹੰਗ
Saa Taa Naa Maa Raa Maa Daa Saa Saa Say So Hang

Saa Taa Naa Maa are the primal sounds that represent the complete cycle of life (also see p. 7).

Saa	Infinity
Taa	Existence
Naa	Death
Maa	Rebirth
Raa	Sun
Maa	Moon
Daa	Earth
Saa	Impersonal Infinity
Saa Say	Totality of Infinity
So	Personal sense of merger and infinity
Hang	Infinity vibrating and real (So Hang – I am Thou)

Self-Realization: Blends our finite with our Infinite reality.

Sat Naaraa-ein Whaa-hay Guroo

ਸਤ ਨਾਰਾਇਣ ਵਾਹਿ ਗੁਰੂ
Sat Naaraa-ein Whaa-hay Guroo

ਹਰੀ ਨਾਰਾਇਣ ਸਤਿ ਨਾਮ
Haree Naaraa-ein Sat Naam

ਸਤ ਨਾਰਾਇਣ ਵਾਹਿ ਗੁਰੂ
Sat Naaraa-ein Whaa-hay Guroo

ਹਰੀ ਨਾਰਾਇਣ ਸਤਿ ਨਾਮ
Haree Naaraa-ein Sat Naam

Sat Narayan is the True Sustainer.

Wahe Guru is indescribable wisdom.

Hari Narayan is creative sustenance.

Sat Nam is True Identity.

Peace: Brings peace and good fortune.

This mantra is chanted to create inner peace so one can project outer peace, happiness, and good fortune. *Narayan* is the aspect of Infinity that relates to the water element. This mantra helps you "go with the flow" and takes you beyond this world to the experience of Infinity.

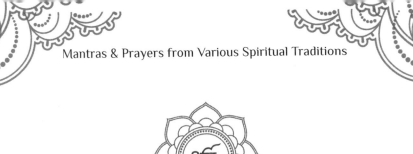

Soft Like Wax

One day when you become soft like wax,

then my thread of life will pass through you,

and out of the accident of the warmth of my heart

one end will get lit.

And you will burn — slowly melting in the heat of the flame.

And when you reach the end,

you will find God waiting for you,

to embrace you into His Infinity.

Eik Ong Kaar Sat Naam Siree Whaa-hay Guroo

Eik Ong Kaar Sat Naam Siree Whaa-hay Guroo:
There is One Creator of the Creation, True is His
Name, Great and Indescribable is His wisdom.

Liberation: Experience the Infinite love of the
Lord through the teacher-student relationship.

Soft Like Wax is a prayer of Yogi Bhajan for his
students to experience Infinity.

Alphabetic Listing of Mantras in this Book

A

E

G

Neutrality: Brings realization of Infinity and takes away duality

N

O

P

The Kundalini Research Institute

KRI's mission is to uphold and preserve the authenticity, integrity, and accuracy of the Teachings of Yogi Bhajan through trainings, research, publishing and resources.

KRI was established in 1972 by Yogi Bhajan.

Find KRI online at
www.KundaliniResearchInstitute.org

KRI's free database of Yogi Bhajan's teachings can be accessed online at

The Yogi Bhajan Library of Teachings™
www.LibraryOfTeachings.org